STRATEGIES FOR INTERPRETING QUALITATIVE DATA

MARTHA S. FELDMAN
University of Michigan

Qualitative Research Methods
Volume 33

SAGE PUBLICATIONS
International Educational and Professional Publisher
Thousand Oaks   London   New Delhi

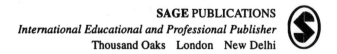

For information address:

 SAGE Publications, Inc.
2455 Teller Road
Thousand Oaks, California 91320

SAGE Publications Ltd.
6 Bonhill Street
London EC2A 4PU
United Kingdom

SAGE Publications India Pvt. Ltd.
M-32 Market
Greater Kailash I
New Delhi 110 048 India

Printed in the United States of America

Library of Congress Cataloging-in-Publication Data

Feldman, Martha S., 1953–
    Strategies for interpreting qualitative data / Martha S. Feldman.
        p. cm. —(Qualitative research methods ; v. 33)
    Includes bibliographical references (p.   ).
    ISBN 0-8039-5915-X. — ISBN 0-8039-5916-8 (pbk.)
    1. Organizational sociology—Research—Case studies. 2. Social sciences—Research—Case studies. 3. Student housing—Michigan—Management—Case Studies. I. Title. II. Series.
HM131.F388 1995
300'.72—dc20   94-23071

95 96 97 98 99 10 9 8 7 6 5 4 3 2 1

Sage Production Editor: Astrid Virding

CONTENTS

Series Editors' Introduction   v

Acknowledgments   vii

1. Introduction   1
   Interpretation Creation   2
   Purpose of This Book   3
   Four Theories   3
   Background Information   6

2. Ethnomethodology   8
   Basic Ideas of Ethnomethodology   9
   Ethnomethodology in Residence Education   12
   Institutional-Level Analysis   14
   An Institutional Reality in Housing   16
   Discovering Norms and Institutional Realities   20
   Summary   20

3. Semiotic Analysis   21
   Semiotic Clustering   22
   Semiotic Chains   30
   Semiotic Squares   33
   Summary   39

4. Dramaturgical Analysis   41
   A Housing Drama   43
   Summary   49

5. Deconstruction   51
   Analysis   53
   Summary   60
   Reflection on Deconstruction   62

6. Conclusion   **64**
      Role of Analysis   64
      Appropriate Uses of the Techniques   65

References   **69**

About the Author   **71**

SERIES EDITORS' INTRODUCTION

Interpretive approaches to field data are diverse, but Martha Feldman has courageously selected four of them, ethnomethodology, semiotics, dramaturgical analysis, and deconstruction, and written a brief overview of their utility. Her presentation is made more compelling because she applies the techniques to aspects of the same body of data drawn from her long-standing and detailed study of a large university housing office. She thus contributes to the number of volumes in the series concerned with interpretive approaches to field data (Ball, Manning, Hunt, Thomas, and others).

She remains close to the data, and keeps a simple format for presenting the approaches. Since the data are from one large study, one see how various facets of a field study can be illuminated and the differential power of the approaches used to reveal answers to central theoretical questions.

In her ethnomethodological analysis, she shows how physical realities (e.g., buildings) become institutional realities and how the latter extends the meanings of the former. In the section on semiotic analyses, she shows how policies help to create the institutional realities and later uses Griemas to show how decisions are differentially perceived by participants. In her dramaturgical analysis, she demonstrates how "backstage" events pattern outcomes, and how decisions are made in well-nested offices deep inside large buildings. Her deconstruction of discussions of salary and reward show how elements of "democracy," and equality are emphasized and hierarchy and power are suppressed. Strengths and weaknesses of the four approaches are evaluated in a final chapter.

Clearly written and well-exemplified, Feldman's book will serve well as a primer on approaches to data for qualitative analysis, whether they be undertaken as "pure" or applied studies done in fields such as evaluation, policy studies, or business.

Peter K. Manning
John Van Maanen
Marc L. Miller

ACKNOWLEDGMENTS

This manuscript has developed through my teaching. I am greatly indebted to the students who have used these techniques. David Bair, Deb Bubro, Ernestine Enomoto, Clare Ginger, P. Roberto Garcia, and Greg Kelly as members of the cult club all helped me begin this work. Ernestine and Clare and Annika Åkerberg, Annelle Eerola, Anna Holm, Simon Holquist, Patrik Kvikant, Juha Lassila, Martin Lindell, Jan Schröder, Caroline Stenbacka, Tiina Vainio, and Niclas Währn from my course in Finland have furthered my understanding of the techniques by their uses of them. I am grateful to Güje Sevon for giving me the opportunity to teach these techniques in Finland.

I am also grateful for the careful readings and helpful comments of Lynn Eden, Elizabeth Hansot, Kathy Knopoff, Alan Levy, Debra Meyerson, Marvin Parnes, Peter K. Manning, and John Van Maanen.

Over the years, I have learned a great deal, especially about semiotics and dramaturgy, by talking with Peter K. Manning and reading his work. My understanding of these theories owes much more to him than I can indicate through citations.

I am indebted to the members of the Housing Office at the university where I pursued my research. They gave freely of their time and knowledge so that I might gain a better understanding of their culture. Concerns about confidentiality prevent me from naming them. I am, however, extremely grateful.

I am deeply indebted to Linda McMichael who did the artwork for this book, and who helps in many ways to make my work life easier and more productive. I am similarly indebted to Hobart Taylor III who helps to make all of my life more joyful.

This book is dedicated to W. Lance Bennett, who introduced me to ethnomethodology and showed me how much fun research could be.

STRATEGIES FOR INTERPRETING QUALITATIVE DATA

MARTHA S. FELDMAN
University of Michigan

1. INTRODUCTION

As I sit in my office up to my eyeballs in data, I am once again impressed with the enormity of the problem of analyzing qualitative data. I have audiotapes, floppy disks, and written documents. I have my field notes and some of my students' field notes. I have copies of reports and minutes of meetings. I have between 10,000 and 20,000 electronic mail messages and another 2,000-3,000 pieces of hard copy mail. I have buttons and calendars and thank you notes. It will take me several weeks working full time just to review all these materials. How am I to make sense of them?

Many people who have worked with ethnographic or other qualitative data will recognize these feelings. The task can be overwhelming. One sometimes feels that reviewing the data only reinforces the complexity and ambiguity of the setting. While it is well to remember this complexity and ambiguity, the task at hand is to create an interpretation of the setting or some feature of it to allow people who have not directly observed the phenomena to have a deeper understanding of them.

Interpretation Creation

The tricky part of this interpretation creation, of course, is to create an interpretation that is neither simply the application of some preexisting theory to your data nor only a description of how the members of a culture understand particular phenomena. Either of these is possible, but often one wants to go beyond these. By the time you have completed fieldwork, you have so much data that, if you were looking to support a particular theory, you probably could. That is not, however, the point of this research. If that is the intended goal, there are much more efficient ways to achieve it. At the same time, the goal is not only to describe a culture. Though describing a culture (or even knowing it well enough to start to describe it) is very difficult and, of course, one cannot describe a culture without also interpreting it (Clifford, 1986), people who do qualitative research are often expected to go quite a bit beyond describing what members know about the culture. The goal, it seems to me, is to develop one's own interpretation of how parts of the culture fit together or influence or relate to one another that is intrinsic to the setting one has studied and, at the same time, sheds light on how similar processes may be occurring in other settings.

If we accept this end, the present problem is how to start. Starting to create an interpretation is like trying to start a jigsaw puzzle that has a million indeterminate pieces. To make this puzzle more confusing, there is no unique solution. That is, one piece may fit with many other pieces. Imagine, in addition, that the picture consists almost entirely of shades of gray (imagine a jigsaw puzzle of a Rothko painting) so that one does not get immediate clues about the fit of the pieces from the picture that forms. (If one were to take this puzzle metaphor too literally, one might think that I am suggesting that there is ultimately a right answer. I am not. While I do not think that all interpretations are equally reasonable or legitimate, I also understand that these concepts—reason and legitimacy—are culturally bounded.)

My experience with ethnographic data suggests that clusters of data tend to stick together. These clusters probably depend on both what is in the researcher's thoughts as the data are gathered and how the members of the culture tend to organize their culture. Some of the challenges at this point of the research involve how to loosen the boundaries of these clusters, how to encourage clusters to interact with one another, and how to access clusters that have potential for interacting. The techniques for data analysis that I describe in this book all have the potential to help the researcher with these challenges.

Purpose of This Book

My purpose in writing this book is to introduce and give examples of some interpretive techniques for analyzing qualitative data. In choosing the four theories that underlie these techniques, I have focused on theories that are oriented to the interpretation of cultures or the context in which actions are taken. In every case I have seen the techniques used, I have been impressed with how much information they allow the author to provide the reader in a relatively succinct manner. I have used each of the techniques with my own data and have been struck by how much more I understand and can communicate about a culture or context after using the techniques. I also like the theories from which these techniques are drawn because they each have relatively few assumptions so that they are applicable to a broad range of phenomena. I do not claim that they are the only useful theories or techniques. Others may be equally or more useful for certain pieces of research. I also recognize that each of the theories I present could be used independently and that each warrants a book of its own. In fact, each has many books devoted solely to it, and I cite many of these books in the text. I find, however, that it is also useful to analyze data from the combined perspective of these theories. As I discuss in Chapter 6, while each of the theories focuses on different aspects of a context, when all four perspectives are combined, the aspects are interrelated in a way that makes the result a rich and textured interpretation of the context. Of course, by focusing on only one of the theories, one can go more deeply into a particular aspect of the context. Individual researchers have to make their decisions about which is more appropriate for their research. In this text, I try to provide the reader with a basic understanding of each of the four theories and some of the techniques for analyzing data that derive from these theories. I provide references so that the reader may pursue in greater depth any of the four theories. I also illustrate the techniques with examples from my own data.

Four Theories

The techniques of analysis I describe are based on ethnomethodology, semiotics, dramaturgy, and deconstruction. All of these theories have assumptions and the researcher must be careful that the assumptions are appropriate to the setting being studied. To my mind, these assumptions are relatively minimal. It is, however, entirely possible that the assumptions do not hold in all contexts. It is therefore important to be aware of them. In this introduction, I briefly describe the main ideas important to each of the techniques. A thorough understanding of the techniques and their appropriate uses is probably best developed through experience. In the following, I attempt to provide a basic understanding by addressing the question of what one is likely to look for and find if one looks through the eyes of an ethnomethodologist, a semiotician, a dramaturgist, or a deconstructionist.

Ethnomethodologists look for *processes* by which people make sense of their interactions and the institutions through which they live. They assume that people do make sense of these phenomena and that their sense making is the basis of their future actions and interpretations (what ethnomethodologists refer to as "going on"). They look for instances in which people have trouble "going on" or for ways in which the "going on" could be problematic but isn't. In other words, ethnomethodologists look for two apparently diametrically opposed situations: breakdowns and situations in which norms are so thoroughly internalized that breakdowns are nearly impossible. Because ethnomethodologists believe that breakdowns are fairly rare, the focus tends to be on widely accepted and taken-for-granted practices. These practices are often characterized by agreement about what is appropriate and tautological explanations of their appropriateness. (For instance, if asked why an action is appropriate, a person might respond that it is the right thing to do.)[1]

A semiotician looks for surface manifestations and the underlying structure that gives meaning to these manifestations. *Denotative* and *connotative* meanings are linguistic terms that are often used in semiotics in relation to surface manifestations and underlying structures. *Denotations* are explicit meanings and *connotations* are implied meanings. For example, the denotative meaning of the word *door* is a "hinged, sliding or revolving barrier that closes an entrance or exit" (*Oxford American Dictionary,* 1980). Its connotation depends on the context. It might connote hidden possibilities, possible linkages, closure, and so forth. Because not all semiotic analyses are of language, the term *surface manifestation* is often substituted for *denotation.* Rather than the word *door*, we may be talking about an actual door. Either the word or the physical manifestation may have connotations or implied meanings depending on the context. An underlying structure is a reasonably coherent set of connotations. The same underlying structure gives meaning to many different denotations or surface manifestations. A person carrying out a dramaturgical analysis is looking for a performance. Standard dramaturgical categories include scene, acts, actors, means, and motives. The primary focus of a dramaturgical analysis is the meaning of a performance for the actors and the audience or potential audience. A dramaturgical analysis has much in common with semiotics. Features of the performance could be considered surface manifestations and the meaning of the performance would be the underlying structure. The dramaturgical approach, however, constrains the focus of analysis to events and draws attention to particular features of an event. Dramaturgical analysis tends to focus on people in their roles and on the intentional strategies they have for producing desired understandings or effects.

A deconstructionist looks for the multiple meanings implicit in a text, conversation, or event. A deconstruction points out both the dominant ideology in the text, conversation, or event and some of the alternative frames that could be used to interpret the text, conversation, or event. Taken-for-granted categories (often in the form of dichotomies) and silences or gaps are elements that support the dominant ideology. Disruptions (sometimes in the form of a slip of the tongue or a joke) are elements that reveal the possibility of other meanings and the instability of the dominant ideology.

In the following chapters, I discuss each of these theories in turn. My objective in these discussions is to provide the readers with sufficient information to be able to use the techniques with their own data. I assume that the techniques will be used after the researcher has in-depth knowledge of the events being studied and the context in which they take place.[2] This knowledge may have been gained through participant-observation or interviews or other data gathering techniques.[3] I also assume that the researcher has data in the form of field notes, interview notes, audio- or visual tapes, hard copy documents, or other forms as appropriate to the setting. I do not specifically talk about ways of managing these data. I assume that the data are used as a record of events and context and also to remind the researcher of aspects of the events or context that she or he has forgotten and to fill in features of the events or context that she or he did not notice at the time of data collection. In this sense, I treat the knowledge of the researcher and the data as coterminous. From this point on, when I

6

use the term *data* I am referring not only to notes or tapes or other tangible objects but also to what the researcher knows as a result of the data gathering process. The analysis I describe, then, is not simply a matter of combining and recombining the recorded or collected data. It also involves using one's knowledge of the setting to determine which of the data are relevant, to have reasons for combining different pieces of data, and, at times, to fill in information that is not in the recorded data. This latter use of one's knowledge is particularly relevant for observational data. Because the recorded data are one's observations and not all observations are recorded at the time field notes are taken, one may find that something one saw but failed to record is a relevant and necessary piece of information.

Background Information

The data I use for the examples are from a four-year case study in the campus Housing Department of a major U.S. state university. The purpose of gathering these data was to understand more about change in organizational routines. By *organizational routines,* I mean repeated organizational actions carried out by two or more interdependent actors. Hiring processes and budgeting processes are examples of such organizational actions. While much of what people do while performing these organizational routines is repeated from previous times, the actors are also often quite sensitive to the context in which they are performing. As the context changes, so may aspects of the routines. Further theoretical background on organizational routines is not included here because the focus is on the techniques of analysis. In this text, I wish to demonstrate how the techniques of analysis can be used to create an interpretation of a setting. The interpretation, then, provides a basis for understanding issues within the setting. For me, for instance, the interpretations provide a base for understanding more about change in organizational routines. I do not talk about my understandings of change in organizational routines in this text. These will appear in a later work (Feldman, forthcoming). The focus here is on understanding the setting in which the routines take place.

The reader does need to know some information about the campus Housing Department to be able to understand the examples. In the following, I provide some basic information. Throughout the text, I give more information as necessary for specific examples.

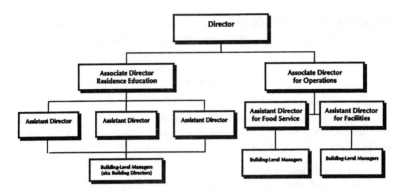

Figure 1.1. Campus Housing Department (partial organizational chart)

In this text, and indeed in everything I write about this department, I focus on specific aspects and necessarily omit others. While I cannot enumerate here the many functions the department serves, I can say that the employees of the department provide a service essential to the university community and that my long period of involvement with the department led me to respect and admire much of the work and most of the people.

The campus Housing Department provides housing for about 10,000 single students and about 1,700 married students and their families. My focus is on the part of the organization that deals with single-student housing. These students reside in approximately 15 buildings or complexes. Each building has three coequal managers. There is one manager in charge of food service, one in charge of maintenance and housekeeping (facilities), and one in charge of Residence Education. (See Figure 1.1.)

Residence education is the major focus of my study. Residence Education consists of an associate director, three assistant directors, and 16 people who report to the assistant directors. Most of these 16 people are the building level managers in charge of Residence Education. They are called building directors, and they manage a staff of from 3 to 40 students (depending on the size of the building) who live in the buildings. These students are called resident directors and resident advisors.

The routines I observed in this organization were the reserves process (a budgeting routine in which approximately 10% of the annual budget is spent), the opening and closing of buildings, and the staff selection process (the process of hiring the approximately 300 resident staff who work for the building directors). I describe these routines in more detail throughout the text as necessary for understanding the use of the analytical techniques.

NOTES

1. In my research with Lance Bennett on jury trials, for instance, we asked people to assess the credibility of stories. There was widespread agreement on which stories were credible. When we asked why a story was credible, people said things like "because it sounded right" or "because it was believable." The task for us as ethnomethodologists, then, was to find out what made a story "sound right."
2. See Agar (1980) and Lofland and Lofland (1984) for excellent discussions of the entire research process for qualitative research.
3. See Agar (1980), Lofland and Lofland (1984), and Spradley (1979) for discussions of data gathering techniques.

2. ETHNOMETHODOLOGY

The fundamental assumption of ethnomethodology is that people within a culture have procedures for making sense. These procedures are "ethno-methods," or culturally based methods. Many of these procedures are verbal. They include telling stories and giving explanations. Other procedures such as the forming of lines (e.g., at a bus stop or a ticket counter) are nonverbal. Ethnomethodologists claim that culture consists of processes for figuring out or giving meaning to the actions of members rather than consisting of a stable set of things that members are supposed to know. The ethnomethodologist's primary focus is on how the norms[1] of a society are developed, maintained, and changed rather than on what those norms are. From this perspective, "the outstanding question for social science . . . is not whether social facts are objectively grounded, but how that objective grounding is accomplished" (Suchman, 1987, p. 57).

Ethnomethodologists are concerned with discovering the underlying processes people use to produce acceptable behavior in a variety of situations. They often study activities that ordinary people engage in without thinking. These include such activities as having conversations, telling stories, waiting in lines, or riding elevators. Sometimes these understandings of daily activities are incorporated into understanding activities that we often think of as more complex and requiring significant expertise. The research Lance Bennett and I did on jury trials is an example of this. First we studied how people listen to stories and decide whether to believe them. Then we showed how this process plays a part in the activity of *doing* justice in a jury trial (Bennett & Feldman, 1981).

Basic Ideas of Ethnomethodology

Ethnomethodology was developed by Harold Garfinkel.[2] Garfinkel's fundamental project involved demonstrating "the researchability and the constraining power of a world organized according to Schutzian [or phenomenological] principles" (Heritage, 1984, p. 74).

The Schutzian principles that Garfinkel was concerned with can be summarized as follows:

1. People will assume things are as they appear to be unless there is some reason to believe otherwise.
2. Actors' knowledge is held in typified form and will necessarily be incomplete. Knowledge is progressively clarified and expanded in the course of action.
3. People engaged in coordinated action assume that others see things as they do. They will actively seek to maintain this shared nature of their knowledge.

Garfinkel undertook to research how we maintain a "world in common" by attempting to disrupt shared "realities." He did this through his "breaching experiments" in which common understandings are violated: Rules of the game are not followed, people ask for clarification of ordinarily well-understood statements or questions, and so on (Garfinkel, 1967). In one experiment, for instance, Garfinkel (1967) asked his students to engage in an ordinary conversation and to insist that the other person "clarify the sense of his common-place remarks" (p. 42). Two of the reported results follow:

Case 1
The subject was telling the experimenter, a member of the subject's car pool, about having a flat tire while going to work the previous day.
(S) I had a flat tire.
(E) What do you mean, you had a flat tire?
She appeared momentarily stunned. Then she answered in a hostile way: "What do you mean, 'What do you mean?' A flat tire is a flat tire. That is what I meant. Nothing special. What a crazy question!"

Case 6

The victim waved his hand cheerily.

(S) How are you?

(E) How am I in regard to what? My health, my finances, my school work, my peace of mind, my . . .?

(S) (Red in the face and suddenly out of control.) Look! I was just trying to be polite. Frankly, I don't give a damn how you are. (Garfinkel, 1967, pp. 42-44)

The failure to take for granted what is ordinarily taken for granted is a breach of the Schutzian principle and, more important, a breach of everyday experience.

Garfinkel found that people quickly become very disturbed by these breaches. The breaches, he suggested, are upsetting because they threaten the very possibility of a shared existence. In later experiments, he demonstrated one of the defenses against this threat by showing how difficult it is for a breach to occur naturally. The consulting experiment was one of these experiments. In it each subject was paired with a counselor who answered the subject's questions with a "yes" or a "no." The counselor consulted a random number table to determine the answer. Subjects were instructed to think out loud about the answers. The transcripts clearly show the subjects' ability to construct a pattern of meaning even out of responses that appear to be directly contradictory to one another (Garfinkel, 1967, pp. 79-94).

Through these experiments, Garfinkel began to demonstrate the flexibility of meaning construction. He showed that all actions have meaning. Both actions consistent with prevailing norms and those inconsistent are meaningful. Deviations from norms are interpreted as motivated and therefore meaningful. These two ideas—that we have ways of producing mutual understanding that are shared and generally acted upon unconsciously and that deviations from these ways are interpreted as motivated, or given meaning—are central to the theory of action developed by Garfinkel. They are also fundamental assumptions of ethnomethodology.

Here the difference between ethnomethodology and earlier theories of social action (à la Parsons, with whom Garfinkel studied) becomes most obvious. Garfinkel rejected the Parsonian notion that people *follow* rules to produce action for a notion that people use rules to interpret and choose actions. In addition, Garfinkel pointed out that this act of interpretation is thoroughly dependent on the context of the action and that every action alters the context. Thus the whole notion of rule becomes inadequate because for each context there would have to be another rule. Because every context is unique and contexts are constantly emerging, there cannot be a set of preexisting rules that are waiting to be followed.

Greetings provide a simple but compelling example of the difference between following a rule and using a rule to choose and interpret actions. Speaking is one form of action. As with other actions, interpretation of speech is context dependent. Speakers assume that listeners are using the context to make sense of what they are saying and that listeners will use whatever context is necessary to make sense of what the speakers say. There is a simple norm in my culture that, if someone greets you, you should greet him or her back. This behavior is often observed. One may also, not infrequently, observe the lack of a returned greeting. If I am greeted by a friend and do not return the greeting, the friend does not necessarily assume that I am either ignorant of or flouting the rule that is supposed to guide my behavior. I may not have heard the greeting either because I am out of earshot or because I am distracted by something else I am thinking about. Or I may have chosen not to return the greeting as a sign that I am angry with my friend. My friend, being aware of these and other possibilities, if she is not otherwise distracted, may interpret my behavior and act according to her understanding of my motivation for not returning the greeting. She may repeat the greeting more loudly if she thinks I am out of earshot; she may chide me with a phrase like "earth to Martha" if she thinks I am being absentminded; she may initiate a discussion of why I am upset or avoid me in the future (depending on her manner of dealing with conflict) if she thinks I am angry. I, in turn, will respond to each of these moves according to my interpretation of what my friend is doing. My interpretation of her behavior is not necessarily related to the reasons for her behavior. I may, in fact, be oblivious to her reasons.[3]

Meaning is created through our actions and our interpretations of our own and each other's actions. Particular actions do not have set meanings. Virtually any meaning is possible. The only absolute in ethnomethodology is that meaning will be made and that the meaning will depend upon how we connect the actions and the context.

Accounts are important in ethnomethodology. One of the principal ways that we understand that someone has perceived a deviation from a norm is when that person asks for an account. In the above example, for instance, my friend may later in the day ask me, "Why didn't you answer me when I said 'hello' to you earlier?" This is a request for an account of my behavior, and it signals to me that I have done something that my friend thinks I should be held accountable for. Consistent with the ethnomethodological perspective on norms, I may have many different reactions to this request for an account. I may agree that one is appropriate and provide one; I may not think that an account is necessary but provide one nonetheless; I may not provide an account; I may provide an account of why I am not providing an account. The possibilities are virtually endless. Again, the only absolute is that each response will have meaning for me and my friend.

Accounts are not always requested. Sometimes people spontaneously provide accounts because they perceive or fear that their behavior or speech will be interpreted in a way other than they wish. They may offer an account to place the behavior in a context that they think is appropriate.

Ethnomethodology in Residence Education

The work of people in Residence Education, particularly the building directors, is intimately involved in developing and maintaining a world in common. The housing of as many as 1,200 students in one building provides many opportunities for the development of norms and for deviations from them. The building directors are the ultimate arbiters of appropriate behavior. While there are rules about what people can and cannot do, whether the rules have been transgressed, by whom, and what is the appropriate response are all matters of interpretation. How does this process of interpretation take place?

The process is one of mutual[4] problem solving, negotiating, and defining. The process, while ongoing continuously, becomes most evident when some person (often the building director or a resident staff member) or group of people (e.g., the residents) announce that behavior they find inappropriate is taking place. A series of conversations ensue in which the participants come to a mutual definition of inappropriate behavior (this may or may not be the same as the behavior originally denounced), including why it is inappropriate, and they negotiate an understanding about future behavior and about ways to remedy any harm to individuals or to the community resulting from the inappropriate behavior. The result is codified in what is called a "behavior contract."

An example of a sort of behavior contract comes from a situation in which a house within the residence hall had used house funds and made

T-shirts that had a picture of a large can of beer along with the name of the residence hall group. This is a violation of the Housing Department's alcohol policy, and it angered many other people who had abided by the rules. The building director describes the interaction as follows:

> I meet with the Resident Director of the house. He is a transfer student from another university and has not understood how seriously the Housing Department enforces the policy regarding the use of house funds to advertise alcohol. He had depended upon the judgment of his government Resident Advisor, a second year staff member, who underplayed my position as well as Housing's position. We discuss the situation and possible remedies. He asks for time to meet with his staff and to get back to me.
>
> The Resident Director meets with his staff who try to talk him out of taking any action. Instead, he asks the government Resident Advisor to meet with me. The government Resident Advisor is in the process of finishing an honors thesis, so our "meetings" take place [through electronic mail]. After a dozen messages and responses, we agree to a solution, and he schedules a meeting with me and the house President and Treasurer, and the Resident Director. . . .
>
> I meet with the group, reiterate Housing policy, and remind them that they had heard all this the previous fall. . . . I also talk about the reasons for the policy. They admit knowledge but cite as examples other houses' shirts from other years. The Resident Advisor notes that the policy is not clearly spelled out in the advisor materials and encourages Housing to include such an explanation. I acknowledge that the Alcohol Policy does not specifically address house shirts and that tradition is difficult to break. I note that the power of folk knowledge which is in opposition to written or spoken policy is one reason that I do not want the shirts to be around next year. We agree on a solution.
>
> All shirts will be sold by the end of the year. If all shirts are not sold, the house officers will cover any advance monies paid to the vendor for the shirts. The house officers will write a letter apologizing for the design on the shirts and for any mixed messages they may have sent to residents or to staff of other houses. They also agree to create posters for the residents of the house explaining in a positive light the actions which have taken place. They agree to see that the poster is placed in conspicuous places in the house and to see that the other officers of the house will understand and support the action agreed upon. (Building Director Role Report, 1989, pp. 23-24)

The process is not always so neat. People do not always agree that they are engaging in inappropriate behavior or that it is any other person's business. Sometimes behavior contracts are made but are not fulfilled.

There are also many other facets of the process that could be explored. Many contingencies arise. A study focusing primarily on this process would elaborate on the ways in which the participants accommodate the contingencies. From an ethnomethodological perspective, the primary interest is in the process. The specifics of the behaviors are less important. Of course, it is very difficult to discuss a process without discussing the context of the process. For this reason, ethnomethodological studies are often rich in substantive details. One must remember, however, that the focus is on how rather than on what.

Institutional-Level Analysis

The dynamics that have been described as taking place in and ordering social interactions are also taking place at an institutional level. That is, not only are people maintaining, elaborating, and altering the local context of their actions, they are also similarly influencing the larger context, or what is sometimes referred to as the structure of their actions. Heritage (1984) claims that "in maintaining, elaborating or transforming their circumstances by their actions, the actors are also simultaneously reproducing, developing or modifying the institutional realities which envelop these actions" (p. 180). While the two levels of context are similar in many ways and the dynamics are the same, the widely shared and taken-for-granted status of institutional realities warrants special attention.

There are many examples of institutional realities. What constitutes an institutional reality in one setting may not do so in another. For instance, gender is widely considered an institutional reality. We take for granted that people can be clearly categorized as male or female and that "other" is not a relevant category. This division of the population is part of the structure of many societies, influencing manners of dress, social interactions, labor force distributions, resource allocation, and more. While the division is neither absolute nor inalterable, it is certainly prevalent and influential.

Examples of institutional realities range from the very consensual to the chronically conflictual. The institution of gender is one about which there is a great deal of consensus (Geertz, 1983, p. 80). It can, nonetheless, be understood as culturally maintained by examining the efforts of people whose gender is, for some reason, problematic. Garfinkel explores this phenomenon in his case study of Agnes, a person with male genitalia claiming to be a woman in order to obtain a sex change operation. As I discuss below, he shows the ways in which Agnes asserted her femininity through her behavior and her accounts of her childhood and the ways in which others (relatives and her boyfriend) created accounts about her gender status. In the case of consensual settings, the issue is how action is produced that is consistent with the perceived rules that will be used for interpreting action.

Chronically conflictual settings include courtrooms and scientific labs in which phenomena are routinely seen and reported very differently by different people. In these cases, the issue is how to account for the discrepancies in such a way that fundamental institutional realities are not disturbed. An institutional reality of the scientific laboratory is that there is such a thing as objective fact. This reality has to be maintained in the light of many discrepant observations. Mulkay and Gilbert (1983) claim, for instance, that "scientists employ asymmetrical accounting to perform interpretative work in such a way that they are able to preserve the underlying assumptions that *genuine* knowledge is immune from non-cognitive influences, and that only one scientific theory is possible in a given area" (pp. 181-182, cited in Heritage, 1984, p. 227). They list a number of ways in which alternate theories and theorists are discounted by the British scientists they studied; among them are "a narrow disciplinary perspective, . . . false intuition, subjective bias, . . . pigheadedness, being out of touch with reality, being American and therefore thinking in a woolly fashion, fear of being discredited with grant-giving bodies, being prevented by disciples from admitting one's mistakes" (p. 176, cited in Heritage, 1984, p. 225).

The really interesting feature of institutional realities from an ethnomethodological perspective is how we maintain them. The assumption is that they must be maintained because they are the basis of social order. The realities are maintained in two general ways. One is that there are actions and behaviors that are consistent with the institutional reality. For instance, if the institutional reality is gender, there are a number of beliefs about how men or women act, how they are similar and different, what kinds of experiences they have had growing up, and so on. A person can maintain the reality by acting in a manner consistent with these beliefs and expectations. When these beliefs and expectations are transgressed, the reality may still be maintained by providing an account of the transgression. For instance, Agnes accounted for her male genitalia as an "accidental append-age stuck on by a cruel trick of fate" (Garfinkel, 1967, pp. 128-129). She claimed never to have had any sexual interest in her male genitalia and, though she was raised as a boy, she claims to have been a boy with feminine tendencies. Accounts do not necessarily have to come from the source of the challenge to the institutional reality. Indeed, other people who knew of Agnes's ambiguous condition had their own ways of ac-counting for it. These ways often involved making a moral judgment about Agnes, but they did not question the fundamental institutional reality that gender is a natural fact upon which social order can be based. Indeed, once she had a sex change operation and was "entirely female," people who had judged her harshly no longer felt the need to, presumably because there was no longer a challenge to the reality of gender that had to be accounted for. In other words, these accounts were all part of the process of, among other things, maintaining the objective reality of sexual status.

Discovering institutional realities is not always easy. They are often taken for granted. When members tell stories, this information is implicit as background knowledge. As Rosaldo (1989) explains, "Ilongot story-tellers no more need repeat what 'everybody' already knows about hunt-ing than a group of avid sports fans need to bore each other by reciting the basic rules of the game" (p. 129). Institutional realities are seldom challenged explicitly by members. Even if they are challenged, the ac-counting mechanisms may be so well developed that members integrate the breach with virtually no acknowledgment of it.

An Institutional Reality in Housing

I had actually completed four years of fieldwork and thought I was through gathering data when I committed a breach that helped me to discover an institutional reality of the organization I was studying. I had agreed to do a series of sessions with Residence Education in the year following formal data gathering. The first session was about boundary spanning and went without a hitch. The second session was designed to supplement the first session and to push the ideas a bit further. (It is probably relevant that I had by that time moved to San Francisco for sabbatical and was only in touch with the director of the organization.) I met with small groups of building directors and suggested we talk about the differences implied by three possible titles for their position—"house mother," "building director," and "residence education coordinator"— and about the organizational boundaries that were relevant to each. I chose these three titles to capture the change from a nonprofessional to a professional position and from a building-centered to an organizationally centered affiliation. The nearest historical precedent to the building director position is the house mother. House mothers were paid to live in the residence hall and look after the students. The responsibilities of these people were different from the responsibilities of either the building directors or the resident staff of today. *In loco parentis* was a guiding principle making the house mother the local parent. She was responsible for no less than the moral, physical, and intellectual well-being of the student residents. Rules about hours, visitation, sexual conduct, moral conduct, and so on were common and were the responsibility of the house mother to articulate and to enforce.

Building director, by contrast, is a professional position requiring a master's degree or the equivalent experience. Building directors do not live in the residence halls. They manage a staff of student advisers and directors who do live in the halls and are available around the clock. Other features of the job have also changed. *In loco parentis* is no longer a guiding principle. Concerns have changed. There is less concern that sex be avoided, for instance, and more concern that residents understand the importance of practicing safer sex. With all these changes, however, they are no less concerned with and often held accountable for the moral, physical, or intellectual well-being of the residents in their buildings.

Though building directors are universally referred to as *building directors,* their official title is *Residence Education Coordinator.* The difference of emphasis in these titles is significant to the building directors. *Building Director* emphasizes the affiliation with the building or specific residence hall. Building directors see themselves as responsible for the well-being of the residents in their buildings and for the development of the community within the building. They subscribe, by and large, to Maslow's theory of a hierarchy of needs in which the "higher" needs of self-actualization and moral development can only be realized if the "lower" needs of safety and security are met. This means that the students must be well-fed, feel secure, and be comfortable in their surroundings. Because the building directors see the success of their work as dependent on these other aspects, they also feel it is their job to make sure these other aspects of residence hall life are well-cared for. Thus everything that goes

18

on in the building is relevant to the building director. The title is appropriate to the image.

The title *Residence Education Coordinator,* by contrast, emphasizes the affiliation with Residence Education and deemphasizes the affiliation with the buildings. It is not entirely clear what such a change would mean. While Residence Education has become increasingly centralized since a new director of Residence Education was hired in 1983, much is still organized around the buildings, and the building directors maintain substantial influence over procedures and decisions. The exercise I proposed to the small groups of building directors was intended to begin developing some ideas about what would be entailed in a role that was less building oriented.

In the first small group meeting, the proposal met with generally tense comments until finally the group leader said that she was feeling a lot of tension and that maybe we should talk about it. At that point the meeting dissolved into a scatter of reactions—some people cried, some people sat silently with pursed lips, some made accusations about me being the boss's lackey and doing his dirty work, and so on. Most of the animosity was related to the notion of a residence education coordinator. The second small group did not react in the same way but was similar to the first in simply going through the motions of the exercise without getting involved or engaged.

My current interpretation of this event is that, in promoting the idea of a role that was defined by the organization (residence education coordinator) rather than by the residential building in which the person worked, I had challenged a basic organizational reality. This reality is that buildings are what residential life is (properly) organized around. By placing the three roles—house mother, building director, and residence education coordinator—in relation to one another, I was suggesting that, as building director was preferable to house mother, so residence education coordinator was preferable to building director. By asking the building directors to think about what their roles would be like if they thought of themselves as residence education coordinators, I was suggesting that they think of their primary affiliation as being with the larger organization—Residence Education—rather than with the buildings they work in. This was contrary to the way these people have traditionally thought of their roles and contrary to their understandings of where their power and job security comes from. It is not only the weight of tradition that makes a building-centered notion of their jobs so important but also their beliefs about the appropriateness of a building-centered perspective. For them, the buildings are analogous to organisms or communities that need someone watching over them to ensure their health and well-being. Taking on the role of residence education coordinator means abdicating their relatively autonomous and locally powerful role to be a cog in the bureaucratic wheel and forsaking the community and all its members. It would be like asking a monarch to give up the throne to be a member of a multinational committee that would rule the country or like asking a parent to give authority for child rearing to a bureaucracy in which she or he would participate.[5]

This breach helped me to realize that the concept of the "building" is an institutional reality of Housing and particularly of Residential Education. This reality is maintained by many beliefs and institutional practices. For instance, there are beliefs that buildings have different characters and different needs (e.g., needs for different accounting systems, equipment, style of furniture, level of maintenance). Each building's budget is presented separately (though the accounting details do not support the easy separation of one building from another), and budget decisions are made by considering each building and its budget separately. Responsibilities are divided by building, not only for the building directors but also for people in other parts of the Housing Department. With building as a central concept, there comes a certain isolation. Every "building" is separate from every other "building" and "buildings" are separate from the central administration.

Some of these *buildings* are not single physical structures as would normally be implied by the term. Combinations of physical structures are sometimes referred to as "buildings." Some combinations are groups of buildings with similar structures, but others are groups of buildings without similar structures. Combinations are all physically proximate, but some structures that are proximate are not combined. Some structures that are combined are small, but not all small structures or even all small, physically proximate structures are combined. In fact, there is no externally observable rule for combining structures into a "building." Thus we see that "building" is a socially constructed concept in this culture and that it is maintained by the beliefs and practices that have developed around the specific structures and combinations of structures that have been designated as "buildings." In the sections that follow on semiotic analysis,

I explore further the building concept and how it is developed in the Residence Education context.

Discovering Norms
and Institutional Realities

How does one begin an ethnomethodological analysis? As mentioned previously, norms and institutional realities are taken for granted. They may be so embedded in the culture of a setting that no one talks about them or is even aware of their existence. This can make it difficult to know how to start.

As illustrated in the previous example, one is sometimes fortunate enough to witness (or cause) a breach. Luck, however, is not the only route to this mode of interpretation. Because a breach may not happen in your presence or may not come readily to mind, you may think about what would constitute unacceptable behavior in this context. Then you need to think about *how* you know that it would be unacceptable behavior. What kinds of cues are given to members, perhaps particularly new members, that help them know how to act? Once you are thinking along these lines, you will probably recognize that the process is not simply socialization in which those who know tell those who don't know *what* they can and cannot do. It is, instead, a much more complex negotiation about what actions mean and which actions fall into what categories. The negotiations can take place through either behavior or speech. The behaviors and speech through which interpretations are made in a particular setting are the "ethno-methods" of that setting.

Summary

The key factor in doing an ethnomethodological analysis is to focus on *how* sense is made rather than on *what* sense is made. Of course, the two are interrelated. Only in the abstract does one have a process without a substance. Any empirical research on the process also requires a deep understanding of the substance. An analysis, however, may emphasize either process or substance. An ethnomethodological analysis emphasizes process.

Remember that you need to consider whether the assumptions of ethno-methodology are appropriate for the research you are doing. The assumptions are as follows:

1. Actions and interactions have meaning for participants. Both following norms and deviating from them are meaningful acts. While the meaning of following norms is often well established, the meanings of deviations often need to be constructed. Meaning may also need to be constructed if no shared norms exist.

2. Participants mutually engage in ethnomethods to construct meaning. The *means* participants use to construct meaning is the primary focus of the ethnomethodologist's attention.

NOTES

1. I follow Heritage in using the term *norm* in reference to constructs that are implicated in the ongoing creation of meaning rather than constructs that determine behavior. Heritage (1984) describes normative accountability as "the grid by reference to which whatever is done will become visible and assessable" (p. 117).

2. This summary draws heavily on John Heritage's book *Garfinkel and Ethnomethodology* (1984). I encourage anyone interested in ethnomethodology to read Heritage's book and Garfinkel's experiments.

3. For another example of the difference between following a rule and using it as a guide to understanding and producing behavior, see Rosaldo's description of Ilongot visits in *Culture and Truth* (1989).

4. My use of the term *mutual* is not meant to imply that the participants have equal power in the process—they don't.

5. The improbability of acquiescence to such a change was no doubt increased by long-standing tensions between the building directors and people higher in the hierarchy to whom the building directors would necessarily be ceding power.

3. SEMIOTIC ANALYSIS

Semiotic theory is defined as "a unified approach to every phenomenon of signification and/or communication" (Eco, 1976, p. 3). "Semiotics is concerned with everything that can be taken as a sign. A sign is everything which can be taken as significantly substituting for something else" (Eco, 1976, p. 7). It is "the study of the signs or systems of signs [and it] concerns the principles by which signification occurs. Signification refers both to the processes by which events, words, behaviors and objects carry meaning for the members of a given community and to the content they convey" (Barley, 1983, p. 394). A key assumption of semiotics is that surface signs are related to an underlying structure. A related assumption is that there is an underlying structure.

Semiotics is fundamentally cultural in its approach. Eco (1976) claims that "semiotics studies all cultural processes *as processes of communication*" and, while he does not claim that semiotics is the only way to study culture, he does say "that the whole of culture should be studied as a communication phenomenon based on signification systems" (pp. 8, 22). Roland Barthes has used the semiotic approach to study such diverse aspects of culture as professional wrestling (1972), the structure of a city, and addresses (1982).

Semiotics is concerned with identifying signs and understanding the processes by which they come to have meaning. The mechanisms most often cited by semioticians as ways of producing meaning are metaphor, metonymy, and opposition. Metaphor and metonymy are similar concepts (Eco, 1976, p. 279). Metonymy involves a relationship between the sign and the signified in which both are in the same domain—the crown stands for the king; both crown and king are in the same domain of meaning. With metaphor, the sign and the signified are not in the same domain—a rose as a sign of love or a crown as the sign of quality. Opposition is a different kind of relationship between the sign and the signified. The sign has meaning because of what it is not. A sign saying "Exit" only has meaning in the context of other signs or other potential signs that say "Entrance." Thus what you are meant to do when you see the sign "Exit" makes sense because of your prior knowledge of the existence of the entrance. In other words, it makes sense only if you know that you are in something. If you didn't know before seeing the sign, in fact, the sign would presumably make you aware that you are in something. This knowledge is fundamental to knowing that you can go out.

Semioticians have devised several techniques that I find useful for interpreting qualitative data. These techniques help one connect the surface indicators to what underlies and gives meaning to these signs.

Semiotic Clustering

The first technique is very simple yet quite powerful. I found this technique in Manning's (1987) book *Semiotics and Fieldwork*. One sets up a table with three columns. The first column is labeled "Competing Meanings" and also can be thought of as denotative meanings or signs. In

Table 3.1 Semiotic Cluster Analysis

Competing Meanings	Connotative Meanings	Institutional Concerns
Buildings. . .		
1. as physical structure	institutions	} legitimation of organizational role } external
2. as residence	home	
3. as community	neighborhood	
4. have reputations	}	
5. have characters	person/organism	legitimation of Building Director role and } external
6. have needs		location of power and control } internal
7. are unique		
8. as field	independent subservient	location of power and control } internal
9. as fiefdom (vested interest)	independent	
10. are autonomous	independent	

this column, one writes all of the various ways one has observed or heard people use the concept of interest. In Manning's case, the concept of interest was "policy"; in my case it is "building." I use the semiotic analysis to deepen my understanding of the institutional reality I became aware of through the previous ethnomethodological analysis. The first step was simply to list the ways that I heard people in Residence Education talk about buildings. Table 3.1, titled "Semiotic Analysis," lists 10 common ways people talked about buildings. They are not listed in order of importance but are grouped by their relations to the other columns.

The second column is labeled "Connotative Meanings." Here the notions of metaphor, metonymy, and opposition are useful. The fundamental question one has to ask oneself is this: "What does it mean when someone in this culture talks about, for example, a building as a community?" This step obviously relies on the researcher's intrinsic understanding of the culture. The technique does not provide the understanding. Rather, it helps to draw many pieces together into a pattern that can increase the significance of the data both to the researcher and to the audience. There is no one right answer in filling out this second column.

In my table, the first three meanings of building (physical structure, residence, community) have connotative meanings based on metonymy. They are all, in fact, meanings closely related to those in the first column but based on my understanding of what it is that Residence Education is trying to create in the residence halls. Within these first three connotative meanings, there is also an opposition that is important for understanding Residence Education. This is the opposition between institution and home/neighborhood. My understanding is that Residence Education is trying to instill in student residents the idea that these buildings are not institutions but are instead the homes and neighborhoods that the students are accustomed to living in. (There will be more on this idea and how Residence Education/Housing helps to produce it later.)

The next four meanings or ways that people in Residence Education talk about buildings (buildings have reputations, buildings have characters, buildings have needs, buildings are unique) are metaphorically related to the notion of a person. The characteristics of being unique and having needs, characters, and reputations all relate to the way we normally think about people. While no one in Residence Education would claim that a building is a person, these personlike qualities are often attributed to the buildings.

The final three meanings (building as field, building as fiefdom or vested interest, and building as autonomous) rely most on opposition. They all relate to how independent or subservient the buildings and the people who run them are. Building as field connects both to independence and to subservience. Field offices receive orders and policies from the central office, but they are also responsible for many local decisions. The subservience is underlined by the metaphoric connection to field slaves (as opposed to house slaves). This connection was noted first by one of the assistant directors of residence education. Metaphorically, the building directors are the field slaves while the central administrators are the house slaves. Field slaves not only were subservient because they were slaves but also had fewer privileges and opportunities than house slaves. Buildings as fiefdoms or vested interests or autonomous is an assertion of the independence of the buildings, though, in raising the issue, the opposite is necessarily implicit (Martin, Feldman, Hatch, & Sitkin, 1983). In other words, the assertion of independence only makes sense where there is a concern about subservience.

The third column is labeled "Institutional Concerns" and involves a leap similar to the one necessary for moving from the first to the second column. This column identifies the issues that are of concern within the organization that relate to the denotative and connotative meanings. This becomes more clear as I explain the specific concerns in the case. The institutional concerns discussed here are not at all obscure. Anyone with more than a casual relationship with Residence Education would recognize these issues as institutional concerns. Again, the table helps not in discovering the concerns but in making clear the connections between them and other features of the culture. In the fourth column, I have simply summarized the institutional concerns as either internal to Residence Education or external. This step is not necessary but simply seems appropriate in this case. In the following, I describe in more detail the institutional concerns and how they relate back to the connotative and denotative meanings.

The most simplified version of these issues is that there is one external and one internal issue. The external issue is the legitimation of the Residence Education role in the Housing Department and particularly the legitimation of the building director role. The internal issue was how centralized or decentralized Residence Education should be or would be. The internal issue has implications for the professionalization of Residence Education and the role of building directors and thus has many possible connections to the external issue.

Legitimation of Residence Education and the building directors in Housing is an issue with many aspects. First, it must be noted that by some measures Residence Education appears to have no problem. The building directors are, for instance, the highest paid and highest ranked professionals in the buildings. They are the only building managers who have secretaries. They have very large student staffs (up to 40). The director of residence education is an associate director of housing whereas the directors of facilities and food service are assistant directors. The director of the Housing Department worked as a building director in the mid-1960s and one of the other associate directors (in addition to the associate director for residence education) worked as an assistant building director in the late 1960s. There would therefore seem to be a lot of support for Residence Education and particularly for building directors.

It is not as simple as that, however. Much of the complication revolves around what Residence Education and building directors should be doing. The director and associate director were building directors during a time when the conception of the job was very different than it is now. It was, at the time, primarily an administrative job with a basically reactive perspective. That is, things would happen (e.g., there would be damage to property or there would be an event in which a resident was in danger or there would be a roommate dispute), and the building director would take care that appropriate actions were taken (e.g., fines were assessed, dangers removed, residents relocated). Nowadays a substantial amount of the building director job is education and counseling; the preferred perspective is proactive; and the issues are multiple and complex. Thus building directors now develop educational programs for such issues as safer sex practices, eating disorders, race relations, homophobia, alcohol and drug abuse, and date rape. Many of these issues are both sensitive and controversial. Building directors must deal with outraged parents, with administrators who have been contacted by outraged parents, and also with upset students for whom these issues may be very relevant.

This shift in the focus of the work has simultaneously increased the amount of work (because the administrative and reactive tasks still have to be done) and raised questions about the legitimacy of the building directors' work. The new kind of building director causes a lot more problems than the old kind.[1] The new kind of building director makes people (including the Housing hierarchy and the university regents) uncomfortable by bringing up sensitive issues, and the building directors are, as a result, a focal point for controversy. On top of all this, the primary work of the building directors is so oriented to the building residents that other employees wonder why the building directors are paid on a 12-month basis while the students are only on campus for a little more than 8 months. The above concerns among others prompted the associate director of residence education to appoint a committee in 1989 to write a report on the role of the building director.

While much of what Residence Education does is done by building directors, the issue of the legitimacy of Residence Education is not just a question of what building directors do. The more general issue is raised by the name itself, Residence Education. What is residence education? What kind of education are we talking about? Clearly, Residence Education must be very careful about the extent to which it treads upon the sacred grounds of academia. While Residence Education does participate in some programs that are academic, it has defined its educational mission as being partly to support academic endeavors and partly to educate people about how to live together. Support for traditional academic endeavors takes the form of libraries and computer centers in the residence halls and academic advising made available in the residence halls. It is very convenient for the students to have these services in the residence halls, but their provision is not a particularly unique contribution to the university. While having these support services in the residence halls makes them capable of being tailored to the needs of residence hall students (most of whom are in the first or second year of school), the basic services are also provided by other parts of the university. What Residence Education claims to do that is truly unique is to help people learn how to live in a community and to help people make the transition from being a child to an adult member of a community. The mission, as stated, is sufficiently unfamiliar that the meaning is quite vague, the means of accomplishing it are unclear, and the measures of success are not established. Thus what distinguishes this organization from all others on campus and legitimates its need to exist and expand is something that is quite ambiguous. It is not surprising, then, that legitimacy is a major issue for Residence Education.

The other major issue highlighted by the analysis is how centralized or decentralized Residence Education should be or would be. This is an internal issue though it is influenced by some external decisions, especially budget decisions. Over the past 10 years, Residence Education has become increasingly centralized. This has occurred, in part, because of an expanded central administrative staff. When the new associate director of residence education was hired in 1983, his central administration staff consisted of one assistant director. Over the next four years, the staff grew to three full-time assistant directors and two full-time clerical staff. The assistant directors have two basic types of duties. One is to supervise people who work at the building level; the other is to coordinate activities that all buildings participate in. (Note: This is a gross oversimplification of the assistant directors' duties but it does capture the essence.) For at least a couple of years, the assistant directors were each in charge of one of the following major areas: hiring (referred to in Residence Education as "selection"), training, and budgeting (referred to in Residence Education as the "reserves process"). In two of these areas—selection and training—the organizational action has become increasingly centralized. This centralization has been made possible, in part, by the presence of a person whose responsibility is to the process rather than to a building and who has the time to devote to changing the process. The centralization has generally though not universally been received very favorably by building directors, but there has been a consistent concern that some control of the process be maintained at the building level. For instance, in the selection process, the initial information meetings and screening process are centralized but they are followed by an interview process that is "individualized" by each building. The training process consists of a similar combination of activities.

One might wonder at this point how either of these issues is connected to the list of competing meanings of buildings. Let us take the issue of Residence Education legitimacy first. That was tied to the meanings of the buildings as physical structure, as residence, and as community. The metaphors associated with these meanings were institution, home, and neighborhood, respectively. While the notion of the buildings as physical structure would not be denied by anyone in Residence Education, it is a concept that is most important as an opposition. These are *not just* physical structures and the inference to institutions is decisively counteracted. In fact, one of the first things most people learn upon coming into contact with Residence Education is that the buildings are not called *dormitories* but *residence halls*. While all of Housing adopts this terminology, Residence Education members are most likely not only to disapprove of the term *dormitory* but also to explain in detail why it is not appropriate. The emphasis here is on the notion of residence—people *live* here. This idea leads naturally to the metaphor of home for a student's room and the connecting halls or building as a whole. Supporting this metaphor, groups of rooms or hallways are often designated as "houses." The rest of the building then becomes the "neighborhood" constituted of adjacent "houses." Residence Education has a particular interest in this terminology vis-à-vis both the residents and the rest of Housing and the university. The notion of residence helps to promote a way of thinking about the buildings that is contrary to the notion of an institution.[2] Institutional notions of housing (e.g., barracks, poor houses, prisons, and detention houses) tend to rely on formal rules rigidly applied to ensure that social order is maintained. This is very different from the methods of maintaining social order in a home or a neighborhood where formal rules (e.g., calling the police) are usually considered to be a last resort. Thus the metaphors of home and neighborhood (or community) help the student residents to invoke some forms of behavior that for many of them are familiar in a setting that is otherwise unfamiliar and could easily invoke alienation and, generally, antisocial behavior. Because Residence Education's particular mission is to help people learn to live together in a community, the metaphors help to put the residents in a frame of mind that promotes what Residence Education is trying to do. The metaphor, presumably, has a similar effect on outside audiences. It legitimates the notion that Residence Education should not just be enforcing rules but should also be helping people deal with the issues (both personal and social) that make it hard to get along with each other.

The meanings associated with the metaphor of buildings as person or organization are relevant to the institutional concerns of both legitimacy and control. The assertion that buildings are unique and have characters, reputations, and good and bad years supports the building director's claim to special expertise. The claim to special expertise is consistent with the fact that building directors tend to specialize in a specific building rather than moving from one building to another. If building directors have special expertise that is specifically associated with the building, then both the legitimacy of their role is sustained and the necessity of a certain amount of decentralization is legitimated.

The issue of power and control is not, however, entirely an issue of the building directors asserting their rights to autonomy. This is reflected in the notion of building as field. Building directors often refer to themselves and are referred to by others as being "in the field" when they are doing their building director duties. Being in the field in most instances (with the possible exception of anthropologists) implies being subservient. Field offices are, for instance, generally not in a policymaking role. People in the field often know more about specific instances and their contexts than do people in the central office (often located in the state or federal capital) yet they are often not allowed to make policies or even decisions about how the instances should be dealt with. While building directors have considerable decision-making power and often have a considerable voice in policymaking, they are subservient to their hierarchical superiors in the central office. They express their frustration at having decisions made by people whom they perceive as knowing less than they do about the situations they are dealing with.

It bears repeating that the semiotic analysis did not lead me to discover facts that I did not already know. It did something much more important, however. It led me to consider relationships that I had not previously acknowledged. How did it do that? I think the answer is fairly simple (but I hope not simplistic). The device illustrated in Semiotic Clustering encourages one to assume that there are connotative meanings and institutional concerns that are associated with the denotative or competing meanings. This assumption, then, leads one to consider what they might be and to see the connections that were formerly obscure. In other words, the device encourages one to dip into different clusters of knowledge (data) so as to fill out all three of the columns. The interpretation comes from the effort to understand the relations among entries within a column or between columns. The usefulness of the device comes from its ability to help the analyst create different interpretations than she or he would have created otherwise. As with any interpretation, the validity of the result is not based on filling out the table but on the usefulness of the interpretation. The primary aim is to be able to make sense out of phenomena that were previously puzzling or to be able to make new sense out of phenomena that were not previously fully examined.

Semiotic Chains

The next two semiotic techniques are useful for exploring features of the issues that have been raised in the previous discussion. The second semiotic technique is the one I have seen most often. Barley's (1983) work on funeral homes provides excellent examples of it. It seems most useful as a map of *how* the underlying structure is produced in everyday signs. To illustrate this technique, I pick up the issue discussed earlier of the difference between a residence hall and a dormitory. As mentioned earlier, in this system the term *dormitory* has been replaced by the term *residence hall*. In the earlier discussion, I suggested that this was part of an effort to create a homelike atmosphere that would be familiar to students and that would encourage them to act in ways that are supportive of the community. In explaining the second semiotic technique, I discuss more about the alternative (the opposition) and about the ways in which either a residence hall or a dormitory might be executed.

First let's discuss the lower part of the diagram. (See Figure 3.1.) This is referred to as the denotative part of the sign system. It consists of visible

31

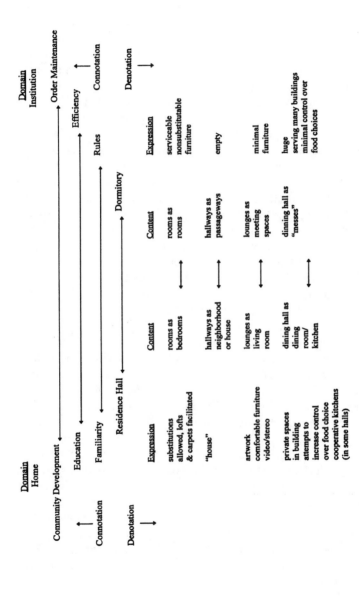

Figure 3.1. Semiotic Chain Analysis

expressions that relate to proposed contents or meanings. On the left-hand side are the expressions and contents relating to the domain of home; on the right-hand side are the expressions and contents relating to the domain of institutions. I have drawn the expressions in the home domain from what I observed in the Housing Department I studied. I have drawn the expressions in the institution domain partly from what they don't want to be like and partly from my own experience of living in a dormitory.

In the home domain, the parts of the building are treated as parts of a house. The students' rooms are bedrooms, which are connected by hallways. Rooms are grouped into "houses," increasing the sense in which hallways are connectors rather than passageways. Lounges are analogous to living rooms and dining halls to dining rooms. These transformations are made possible by policies that allow students to substitute their own furniture for the institutional furniture provided. Storage is available for the institutional furniture. Students are allowed to build "lofts" that dramatically increase the amount of usable space by raising their beds above their heads. In fact, housing has even facilitated lofts by working out deals with companies that put them up and take them down for the students. Similarly, Housing has made it easy for students to buy carpets that give their rooms a homier look. The lounges are made into living rooms by the addition of artwork and video and stereo equipment as well as by general concern with the quality, design, and comfortableness of the furniture. Dining halls are moved in the direction of dining rooms or kitchens by having small private spaces in the dining hall, by having dining halls in every building and cooperative kitchens in some buildings. A more homey atmosphere is also encouraged by increasing the amount of control over food choice. Dining halls have salad bars with many choices and a range of options that allow people to exercise some control over their diet. All dining halls, for example, serve vegetarian entrées.

By contrast, the institutional approach focuses more on maintaining order and efficiently providing room and board. Rooms are furnished with serviceable, nonsubstitutable furniture. In the extreme, furniture may be bolted down. Hallways have no particular significance. Lounges are primarily meeting spaces with minimal furniture, and dining halls or messes are huge, may serve more than one building, and provide minimal choice of food. This characterization is fairly extreme and much institutional housing may fall somewhere between this extreme and the residence hall environment described on the other side of the diagram.

The upper part of the diagram contains the connotative meanings. These are the implicit meanings, or what is signified by the signs in the lower part of the diagram. These meanings are produced by the contents and expressions in the lower part of the diagram. (Of course, the implicit meanings also produce the explicit signs in that people committed to these meanings create policies that promote them.)

On the left-hand or "home" side, the ultimate value is community development. This is supported by a commitment to educating people about ways of living in a community that focuses on familiarity. The notion is that, by understanding more about oneself and about other people, one is better able to be a part of the community. The use of *familiarity* is a pun in that it means both connecting with the people who are currently in the community and connecting with the ways of behaving that are already known from having lived in communities prior to attending the university. All of these meanings are implicit in the term *residence hall* and in the specific contents and expressions described in the diagram.

By contrast, the ultimate value relating to the dormitory concept (as a defining opposition to residence hall) is the maintenance of order. The efficient provision of contracted services is coupled with an expectation of strict adherence to rules. The connotations here have the feel of an exchange relationship. The institution provides services in exchange for which the students follow rules. The relationship is distant and formal. If the contract is broken (i.e., students break rules), then the relationship is severed (i.e., residents are evicted).

Semiotic Squares

The third semiotic technique is called a semiotic square. It was developed by Greimas (1987) and is described in a book of his essays titled *On Meaning*. A semiotic square describes a system of rules or a grammar through which meaning is produced. The grammar Greimas describes is based on opposition. It consists of four basic elements: things that are prescribed, things that are prohibited, things that are not prescribed, and things that are not prohibited.[3] Take, for instance, the grammar of a language. In American English, there are rules about what one needs to do to produce a grammatical sentence (e.g., there should be noun-verb agreement) and there are rules about what does not produce a grammatical sentence (e.g., in most cases, having either a noun or a verb missing—referred to as an

34

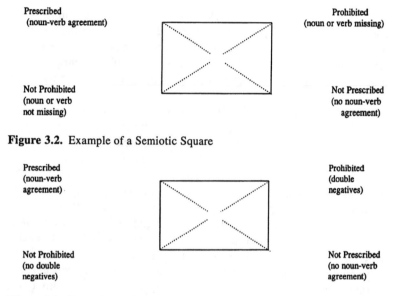

Prescribed
(noun-verb agreement)

Prohibited
(noun or verb missing)

Not Prohibited
(noun or verb
not missing)

Not Prescribed
(no noun-verb
agreement)

Figure 3.2. Example of a Semiotic Square

Prescribed
(noun-verb
agreement)

Prohibited
(double
negatives)

Not Prohibited
(no double
negatives)

Not Prescribed
(no noun-verb
agreement)

Figure 3.3. Example of a Failed Semiotic Square

incomplete sentence).[4] The contradictories of these two rules are that which is not prescribed (e.g., having noun-verb disagreement) and that which is not prohibited (e.g., having both a noun and a verb in a sentence). A semiotic square diagrams this set of rules. See Figure 3.2. On the top of the square are the prescription (upper left) and the prohibition (upper right). On the bottom of the square are the nonprescription (lower right) and the nonprohibition (lower left). The diagonal relations are called contradictions. They are direct opposites and cannot both exist simultaneously. The horizontal relations are contraries. They may both be able to exist but, particularly for the top horizontal relation, only with a great deal of tension. The elements in the square are also related vertically. Elements connected with a vertical line are said to imply one another. Thus, in most cases, noun-verb agreement implies that neither the noun nor the verb is missing, and the noun or verb missing implies their lack of agreement.[5]

While there are lots of rules about how to make grammatical sentences in American English, not all rules can go on the same square because of these requirements for vertical, horizontal, and diagonal relations. Take, for example, Figure 3.3. We start with the same prescription as in

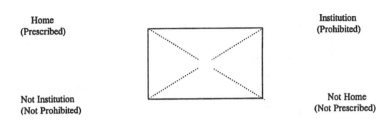

Figure 3.4. The Home-Institution Relationship

Figure 3.2, but we change the prohibition. Noun-verb agreement is the prescription and not using double negatives is the prohibition. Their contradictories are on the diagonals. These are valid rules of American English.
There is, however, no tension between these two in the horizontal relations
and there is no implication in the vertical relations. Figure 3.3 is a failed
semiotic square.[6] Note that the successful square allows us not only to
map our knowledge of the system of rules but also to elaborate on the
relations among the rules. This happens particularly in the vertical relations or implications between what is prescribed and not prohibited and
between what is prohibited and not prescribed. The failed square, by
contrast, simply maps out what we already know about what is prohibited
and what is prescribed. The vertical relations provide no new insights.

We can use a semiotic square to explore further the home-institution
relation discussed in the second semiotic analysis. Home is the prescription;
institution is the prohibition. The square (Figure 3.4) helps us to see that,
in this system of rules or meaning, "home" implies "not institution" and
"institution" implies "not home." The more one emphasizes home, the more
one deemphasizes institution. Thus any action within this system of rules
has a double meaning; if it promotes home, it demotes institution and vice
versa.

Another way the squares can be used is to map systems of rules in different domains. Greimas (1987, pp. 52-56) does this by mapping sexual
relations in the cultural, economic, and personal spheres. In my research,
different domains may be different parts of an organization—units or
hierarchical levels, for instance. To illustrate this use of semiotic squares,
I need first to describe briefly another routine in Housing. It is called the
reserves process. It is a budgeting routine that allocates about 10% of the
budget to specific projects within each residence hall.[7] Over the years, I

have observed the routine of the Residence Education and Facilities directors trying to get the managers at the building level to submit to them a list of projects the building-level managers all agree on for their buildings. Over the four years I observed the routine, the administrators tried several different means of obtaining these lists, which they refer to as consensus lists. They exhorted people, they changed forms, they asked for inclusive project lists rather than just lists of projects that could be funded within the available budget. These efforts produced little change. For the most part, buildings that had submitted consensus lists in the past continued to do so and buildings that hadn't didn't. Changes in personnel seemed to have the largest effects in either direction. Sometimes people in Residence Education would report that they had a consensus list in their building but, when the actual budget meetings took place, there would be two lists from that building. As I observed this process, I found it very puzzling that such a little change with so much high-level support could not be brought about.

Of course, one possibility is that it isn't a little change at all and that producing a consensus list would, in fact, cause dramatic changes in the interactions and power dynamics at the building level. While this is possible, the fact that some buildings did submit consensus lists suggests that there is nothing intrinsic in the roles of the managers that would impede such coordination.

I started to explore this question by mapping out a semiotic square that describes the prescription the central administrators support vis-à-vis their subordinates' positions in the reserves process (see Figure 3.5). What they are asking people to do is to focus on their building affiliation rather than their organizational affiliation. Thus the phrase *buildingwide consensus* is in the upper-left corner as the prescription and the phrase *organizational affiliation* is in the upper-right corner as the prohibition. Their contradictories are on the diagonals. Note that buildingwide consensus within this set of rules implies not focusing on organizational affiliation.

The notion of a narrative that underlies the semiotic squares led me to the next step in this analysis. The narrative is based on the chronological story of the reserves process. The story begins with a period of the central administration giving out information and instructions to the building-level people. Then there is a period of building-level meetings and the buildings give information back to the administrators about what projects they would like to have funded. These parts of the process are represented by square A in Figure 3.5. Following these steps, there is a period of

37

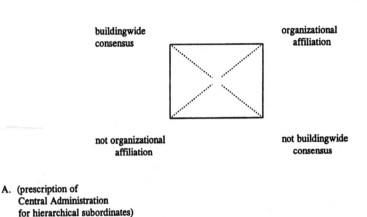

buildingwide
consensus

organizational
affiliation

not organizational
affiliation

not buildingwide
consensus

A. (prescription of
Central Administration
for hierarchical subordinates)

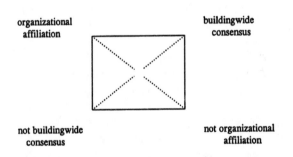

organizational
affiliation

buildingwide
consensus

not buildingwide
consensus

not organizational
affiliation

B. (prescription of
Central Administration
during resolution process)

Figure 3.5. Semiotic Square Analysis

meetings in which the central administrators make decisions about which
projects will be funded. These meetings also need a square.

The meetings among the central administrators followed a fairly similar pattern during the four years I observed them. In general, each building was taken up in turn and projects were considered one by one for the building under consideration. While most of the projects came from the lists provided by building managers, some projects were submitted by other sources, mostly within Facilities. There were always more projects than could be funded. The most common means of dealing with the scarcity of resources was for the person running the meeting to ask the representatives of Facilities and Residence Education each to give up some project. They would take turns giving up projects until the budget was within a reasonable range. While this procedure required considerable cooperation and goodwill, it did violate the assumption of a common interest in the projects that underlies a consensus list.

At this juncture in the process, organizational affiliation takes precedence and the buildingwide consensus becomes unimportant. This part of the process is represented in square B. It belies the rhetoric of the central administrators vis-à-vis the consensus lists. While the administrators may very consistently support the idea of consensus lists, the fact that they are so easily able to move away from the notion of consensus projects suggests that it is not hard for them (and presumably for their subordinates) to distinguish what is important to Facilities from what is important to Residence Education. (Because the procedure is one of giving up projects, it may be more appropriate to say that one can distinguish what is unimportant to Facilities from what is unimportant to Residence Education.)

When we compare squares A and B, we see that what is prescribed in one part of the process is "prohibited" in another. The hierarchical relationship between the parts of the organization represented by these squares influences the nature of the conflict. In this case, square A represents the rules the hierarchical subordinates are supposed to follow while square B represents the rules the hierarchical superiors follow (at least in part of the decision process). When the grammar of a hierarchically superior part of the organization is different than that of a hierarchically subordinate part of the organization, the conflict can result in transgression or alienation or both (Greimas, 1987, p. 59).[8] A transgression (not submitting consensus lists) is what we are trying to explain. The discrepancy in rules represented by the semiotic squares provides an explanation. The hierarchical subordinates are following the rules represented in square B rather than those in square A. They are, in fact, following the example of their hierarchical superiors rather than doing as they are told. The discrepancy may also help to explain the considerable alienation observed in this process. The alienation is often expressed in the form of cynicism by people at the building level about the efforts they make to provide information to the administrators and the extent to which the information is used. The analysis can also be extended to more than two parts of an organization. The number and power of parts of the organization that are supportive or not of a particular relation will indicate but not determine whether the relation will occur and will provide a way of understanding reactions to the relation when it does (or does not) occur.

Summary

In this section, I have presented three techniques for doing semiotic analyses. Each of them was useful for illuminating different aspects of the organizational culture I have studied. In all cases, I provided the observations and I knew the observations before doing the analyses. In all cases, the devices helped me to see relationships that I had not been aware of before doing the analysis. This is why I use the term *illuminate*. Using the devices is like casting a flashlight in a dark corner. One sees things that one could not see before. I am not so naive, however, as to believe wholeheartedly that the relationships are just there waiting to be discovered. I know that considerable effort goes into working out sensible interpretations once the connections are "lit up." This work of creating interpretations is, however, something that we all do in everyday life without even being particularly aware of the act. The problem, it seems to me, is not learning how to create interpretations but being able to create interpretations that make new sense of known phenomena or that combine phenomena in new ways. I find these devices particularly useful for this purpose.

Each device helped to create interpretations about different aspects of the organizational culture. The first analysis was particularly useful for illuminating the big picture. By starting out with how people talk about buildings, which I had already determined was a central reality through the ethnomethodological analysis, I was able to understand how the institutional concerns were invoked through seemingly mundane conversations. Not only was I, as a result, able to develop new interpretations concerning the relations of phenomena within and between columns, but I also am able to use this new understanding in future interpretations. That is, when

I listen to a taped discussion or read my field notes, I have a new stock of knowledge about what people might be saying when they talk about buildings.

The second device is particularly useful for examining *how* a culture manifests a particular opposition. In this case, for example, it helped to show how the organization tries to establish the residence halls as homes rather than as institutions. This particular opposition gives meaning to the acts and policies that are observed in the setting for both participants and observers. For instance, the ability to substitute one's own furniture for the furniture provided could have many meanings. In a rented apartment, for instance, it would be considered a right and the denial of this right is what would be particularly significant. The possibility of institutional rules in the context of the residence hall is what helps give it the particular meaning of homeyness. The device used for the second semiotic analysis is especially useful for focusing on a relationship of opposition and exploring how the opposition gives meaning to specific acts and policies.

The third device also emphasizes opposition and is used by some to discover and discuss the oppositions (Enomoto, 1993; Fiol, 1989). While I find it useful for this purpose, I think its greatest use is in exploring the differences between sets of rules at different levels or in different parts of an organization. A narrative about what actions are being taken by whom is useful for this technique. The relevant oppositions can, then, be diagrammed for the actors in each phase of the narrative. This adds information about the narrative. In my case, it suggested an entirely new possible explanation for a paradox in the narrative.

Many researchers may be able to use all three devices to aid in constructing interpretations. Some of the devices, however, may not be appropriate for certain sets of data. Using all of them is not of any particular importance. What is important is to use them in ways that aid in gaining new understandings and to be aware of the assumptions you are making in using these techniques.

The devices are somewhat coercive. They work on the assumption that there are underlying relationships between denotative phenomena, or signs, and connotative phenomena, or meanings. They assume that there is an underlying structure and that the signs are manifestations of it. They assume that opposition is an important element in underlying structures. If you do not believe that this is true of the culture you are studying, you should not use these devices. In this matter, the researcher has to rely on her or his common sense and understanding of the culture and of semiotics. The devices cannot reflect on their own appropriateness.

NOTES

1. The new kind of building director would claim that the problems are there and that it is better to deal with them proactively.

2. In this section, I use the word *institution* to refer to a particular approach to housing. It is unlike the use of the term in other parts of this text.

3. Greimas's terms for the oppositions involved are *contradictories* and *contraries*. A *contradictory* is a true opposite. A *contrary* is an opposing relationship also referred to as a *homologous contradictory*. That which is not prescribed is the contradictory of that which is prescribed. That which is prohibited is the contrary of that which is prescribed.

4. Note that, in this case, that which is prescribed and that which is prohibited could be reversed if the rules were worded differently. That is, having both a noun and a verb is prescribed and having noun-verb disagreement is prohibited.

5. The most common example of where this is not the case is where the subject is implied, as in a command (e.g., "Close the door") in which the implied subject is "you."

6. The idea of a failed semiotic square occurred to me as a way of thinking about the constraints on the choice of the contraries on the top horizontal line.

7. I provide only the details necessary for understanding the semiotic analysis here. More details are available in Feldman (forthcoming).

8. Of course, the extent of alienation depends on the extent to which the hierarchical subordinates rely on the approval or acceptance of their hierarchical superiors or the extent to which the hierarchy defines the larger society.

4. DRAMATURGICAL ANALYSIS

As the name suggests, the central principle of this form of analysis is the concept of the drama. Life is a stage upon which performers play. The public performances they make (where public is what is done in the presence of other people or that affects other people—in other words, most acts are public) are what produce meaning. Thus meaning is produced in action. While dramaturgical analysis is generally used to explicate very public performances such as organizational rituals, it can also be used to understand relatively private performances such as the execution of parental roles. The analysis includes not only the act itself but also and, more important, the meaning produced by the act or the messages that are conveyed by the act.

Dramaturgical analyses may focus on the display or they may focus on what makes up the display. For instance, some dramaturgical analyses are about the meaning of public presentations or ceremonies such as the police funeral or the publication of arrest statistics (Manning, 1977). Other dramaturgical analyses focus on the elements of these performances such as the roles people are playing and the setting in which they are played. Burke's pentad of social action fits this latter sense of dramaturgical analysis. It divides social action into five basic elements: scene, act, agent, agency, and purpose (Burke, 1969). Of course, some analyses combine both the public performance and the elements that make it up. Erving Goffman (1959, 1967, 1974) is one of the best known users of the dramaturgical approach to sociological phenomena. He focused particularly on the concepts of role playing or role taking, front and back stages, ritual, and the control of meaning.

Dramaturgical analysis tends to have a functional tone to it. The observation that dramas serve certain purposes should not, however, be taken to imply either that these purposes are necessary or that the particular means of fulfilling the purpose is the only way (Manning, 1992). For example, the budget (reserves) meetings discussed in the section on semiotic squares serve a number of symbolic purposes. They establish the authority and decision-making status of the people who attend them. They express the unity of concern about the buildings by the various organizational units (e.g., Facilities, Food Service, Residence Education). This concern for the buildings helps to draw the parts of the organization together with a common purpose. This sense of common purpose helps to legitimate all of the units. This legitimation may be most helpful to Residence Education because its purpose is the most ambiguous. These symbolic purposes are not, however, necessarily essential to the organization and these meetings are not the only way to accomplish these ends.

Fundamental to doing a dramaturgical analysis is the question of what performance is taking place or what meaning is being portrayed to an audience and how the elements that make up the performance contribute to that meaning. Burke's five elements are very useful in this process. The scene is the setting of the performance, the act is what is done during the performance, the agent includes the actors and the roles that they play, the agency is the means through which the agents bring about their actions, and the purpose is the reason or motive for the performance. I find it helpful to consider explicitly the audience as well given that a performance may have many audiences and the meaning may be different for each.

A Housing Drama

The reserves meetings held every year in November are an event appropriate for a dramaturgical analysis. While they are witnessed directly only by those attending the meetings, they provide an arena for a performance that has meaning to both hierarchical subordinates and superiors. The director of the Housing Department, the only central administrator who does not attend the meetings, receives the budget decisions and gives final approval (or disapproval). The subordinates (e.g., building-level managers) are aware of the performance, in part, because they provide many of the props (in the form of information). They also await the outcome of the performance. The instrumental purpose of the reserves meetings is to determine how approximately 10% of the budget will be spent. This 10% is used for furniture, equipment, maintenance, and renovations in buildings. Removing asbestos, replacing elevators, buying mattresses, resealing doors, carpeting hallways, creating a snack bar, renovating a dining hall, reupholstering lounge furniture, buying artwork and audiovisual equipment are all examples of specific projects funded through the reserves process. These projects often make a substantial difference in the living conditions, infrastructure, and appearance of the buildings. They tend to make the buildings easier to maintain and clean both because new things don't break as easily and because residents tend to be more careful when the appearance is aesthetically pleasing. The projects also help to support the community development goals of Residence Education. Some projects (e.g., buying audiovisual equipment) directly support the programming efforts of Residence Education. Other projects (e.g., new lounge furniture or artwork for lounges) help create spaces conducive to effective programs.

The participants in the meetings are the associate directors for Residence Education and for Operations, and the assistant directors of Facilities and Food Service and the administrative manager. In the last year I observed these meetings, an assistant director of Residence Education also attended. The assistant directors of Facilities and Food Service and the administrative manager report to the associate director of Operations so their immediate supervisor is in the room. The organizational chart (see Figure 4.1) shows the people who attend the meeting. (The director of the

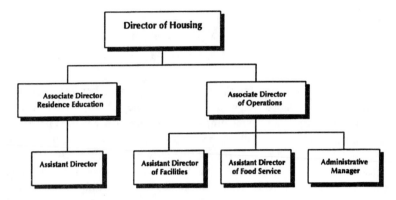

Figure 4.1. Organizational Chart of Reserves Meeting Participants

Housing Department is on this chart even though he does not attend the meeting.) In the following description, I refer to these people by their titles or their actual gender pronouns.

The assistant director for Facilities is probably the most active participant. He will oversee most of the projects that are approved. He also does a yearly maintenance audit of each building that surfaces some of the major projects like reroofing or asbestos removal that may not be obvious even to people working in the buildings. In the first meeting of every year, he summarizes the major projects that he feels need to be undertaken, and he often provides background information on these projects and sometimes provides information about projects that were approved the year before.

The director of Food Service is generally not very active. The budget requests for Food Service are relatively separate from the other units. Also, the director of Food Service for the first three years of observation preferred to negotiate expenditures separately with the director of the Housing Department. In the last year of observation, a new director of Food Service had been appointed. It appeared that he would be a more active participant but he felt he needed to observe for the first year.

The administrative manager is an accountant. He is mostly concerned with how much is being spent and with keeping total expenditures within budget. He often tries to find ways to reduce the cost of particular projects. He consistently objects to any project that involves borrowing money or drawing down savings. He often suggests the pursuit of other sources of funds for projects.

The associate director for Operations runs the meetings. He sits at the head of the table with the administrative manager at his side. He schedules the meetings and keeps them moving at a pace that will accomplish the task within the allotted time. He knows little about the specific projects proposed or about the condition of buildings, but he has been in Housing since the late 1960s and has been involved in the reserves process since 1984. Thus he provides lots of information (not all of it correct) about when something was last done or how much something ought to cost or how a particular space has been used and so forth. He also has a closer relationship with the director of Housing than anyone else, and he speculates about what projects the director is unlikely to approve, mostly due to cost.

The associate director for Residence Education plays two roles. He occasionally weighs in on a specific project that is particularly important to Residence Education or to a building director, the librarian, or the person who runs the computing centers. Most of the time, however, he plays a kind of "outsider" role. He does this by asking general questions about why a project costs a certain amount or about whether it would make sense to spend more and get a better project or about whether a project can or should be put off for another year. His questions often surface assumptions that may be held in common by the director of Facilities and his boss. While these assumptions often turn out to be valid, occasionally the questions result in a new way of thinking about a project.

The assistant director for Residence Education the one year she attended participated mostly as a Residence Education partisan. She and her boss had discussed a strategy of pulling together projects from several buildings that had an academic aspect to them (e.g., equipment and furniture for libraries) and suggesting funding these projects as a package rather than as individual projects in each building. Her role was specifically to argue for this package. Everyone agreed early on that the package should be funded. (The administrative manager also suggested going to the regents with a proposal for increasing the rates by the amount needed to cover this package.) This left little for her to do but observe. This observation was useful for two reasons. One is that she, like the new Food Service director, intended to be more active in future years. The other is that she would be working with the people who report to her on what kind of information is needed to support these meetings. In fact, she and the directors of Facilities and Food Service held several meetings later in the year to discuss how to get their subordinates to provide better and more timely information and how to get them to work better together.

The audience for this performance is twofold. There are the people who are not in the meeting. These include the director of the Housing Department and the building-level managers in Residence Education, Food Service, and Facilities. All of these people await the outcome of the meetings to pass their judgment and deal with the outcome. The director of the Housing Department must decide whether he agrees with the decisions and how much revision he will request. The building-level managers' lives over the next year (or more) will be considerably influenced by the decisions. They assess the effectiveness of their hierarchical superiors by the decisions that are reached.

Everyone in the meeting is also audience. Each person is displaying to every other what it means to be in her or his particular role. Hierarchical position seems to be important. The two associate directors, for example, do not, for the most part, play partisan roles. The associate director for Residence Education has had to be partisan some of the time in the past, but the participation of the assistant director may reduce the necessity for that. In fact, it is possible that part of the reason for the attendance of the assistant director for Residence Education is that the associate director wants to play a more equal role vis-à-vis the other associate director. It certainly makes the relationship more symmetrical. The assistant director for Facilities and the administrative manager (and we may assume the assistant director for Residence Education and Food Service in the future) perform more narrowly focused roles. While they express concerns for the system as a whole, the primary focus of the Facilities director is the integrity of the buildings and the primary focus of the administrative manager is the integrity of the budget.

In considering the dramaturgical nature of these meetings, one of the features that stands out is the location, or scene, of the meetings. They take place in the conference room of the central administration building. This room is at the very back of a large rectangular space. The main entrance to the space is at one end of the rectangle. There is a receptionist at this entrance who asks visitors what their business is. After the receptionist's desk, the space broadens. There are offices on both sides of the space with alcoves for secretaries outside these offices in the interior of the rectangle. Photocopying machines and filing cabinets are located at intervals in the middle (width wise) of the rectangle. It is impossible to walk in a straight line from the receptionist's desk to the conference room. At several points en route, one feels as if one is about to walk into someone's office and may be asked if one needs help. At the end of the walk, one is in a narrow corridor with an office door, which is almost always open, to the right and the conference room door, which is often closed, to the left. Again, the people in the room with the open door often ask if one needs help. (See the floor plan in Figure 4.2.) One does not arrive at the conference room by accident. The conference room is located next to the director of Housing's office. There are windows at ceiling level on one side of the room that open onto the director's office. One cannot see into his office (unless one were to stand on a chair or ladder), but when meetings are held in the late afternoon, the participants often remark upon the director's departure when the lights go off in his office promptly at 4:30. On an adjacent wall are wooden bookshelves. The opposite side of the room has windows that open onto the street. Most of the room is filled with a large oval wood conference table. The wood is beautiful and appears to be expensive. There are 10 large chairs around the table. The chairs are luxurious. They are upholstered in gray-blue material with wooden bases; they have high backs; they swivel, roll, and tilt. One feels important in this room. One also feels insulated in this room.

The reserves meetings take place in this room so removed, both literally and figuratively, from the buildings that are the subject of the meetings. The participants (with one exception in the last year) all have their offices in the rectangular space outside the conference room. During the meetings, there are often questions about the size or configuration or condition of a particular space in a residence hall. Occasionally someone will call one of the building managers either during the meeting or between meetings. This is an extremely rare occurrence—certainly fewer than 5% of all questions are dealt with in this way; probably fewer than 1%. Most questions are resolved by guessing. This is not a disparaging remark. These guesses are often quite sufficient and always less time consuming than requesting further information.

The meetings also feel remote to the people in the buildings who provide information and are the recipients of the decisions. The building directors complain that they have no idea about the basis of the decisions. The process is a mystery to them.[1]

48

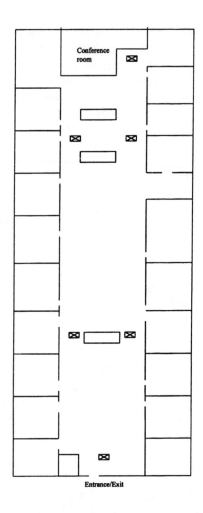

Figure 4.2. Floor Plan

NOTE: The area is approximately 105 × 45 feet (a standard office is approximately 9 × 12 feet)

The entire scenario is reminiscent of *The Wizard of Oz*. The meetings take place in a room that is very removed and hard to get to. Decisions emerge from this place and transform reality as if by magic. It is not clear how things done outside the room (information given) relate to the things done inside the room. The effect is to enhance the appearance of power of the people inside the room. Yet when one is inside (behind the wizard's curtain), the decision-making process seems quite ordinary and the isolation of the decision makers quite unnecessary for making these decisions. Perhaps the main difference is that there is no one who is likely to play the role of the dog Toto and pull back the curtain to reveal the wizard to be an ordinary person.

Summary

Again, the strength of the dramaturgical analysis rests on two features. One is the categories it proposes for organizing observations. The other is the assumption that there is a performance going on and that the performance has meaning for people participating in and observing the performance. I basically used the categories proposed in Burke's (1969) pentad. First, I described the instrumental purpose of the meetings, having earlier reflected on the possible symbolic purposes. The category I used was the act. I described the focus of the reserves meetings and the sort of decisions that are made in the meetings. Then, I described who participated (the agents) and discussed in some detail the role that each participant played. Next, I discussed the audience. This is a category that is not included in Burke's pentad but is implicit in the whole notion of dramaturgy. Thinking about who the actors might be performing for is important for attributing meaning to the performance. Indeed, the comparison with *The Wizard of Oz* drama is only relevant from the perspective of the hierarchical subordinates in the audience. Finally, I considered the setting. I did not explicitly consider agency or purpose. Upon reflection, it seems clear that the means (agency) for bringing about the performance, the isolation, and, indeed, the decisions is the authority vested in each of these people by virtue of their organizational position. Without this authority, the performance, isolation, and decisions would not have the same significance.

This use of the dramaturgical categories to organize my operation created for me an impression that reminded me very much of another drama—*The Wizard of Oz*. The similarity is first suggested by the isolation of the setting and the difficulties in getting to the place where decisions are made. The comparison is sustained by the impact of the decisions that emanate from this place on the supplicants who are excluded from the decision process. The lack of control over decisions and the lack of fit between input and output increases the mystery of the decisions. The final similarity between the reserves drama and *The Wizard of Oz* is the ordinariness of the people making things happen—the wizard in the fictional drama and the decision makers in the Housing drama. Here, in fact, the fictional drama and the Housing drama diverge slightly. The decision makers in Housing actually do have the power to make some things happen. But the fictional drama and the Housing drama are still similar in that the mystification of the decision-making process increases expectations beyond what actually can be delivered.

My observations of the reserves process had mostly been of people engaged in relatively mundane practices: estimating the cost of new shower stalls, weighing the importance of new lounge furniture against replacing hallway carpet, and thinking about whether all this can be done within time and financial constraints. It was only when I looked at these observations through the categories imposed by the dramaturgical analysis that I began to create an interpretation that connected the ordinariness of these actors and the acts that take place in the conference room with the mystification and helplessness felt by the people who witness and receive the performance.

As with the other analyses, it should be clear that the interpretation I have begun here is just one of many possible. It draws on certain features of the phenomenon and not on others. Its validity does not come from the ability to use the dramaturgical categories but from its ability to help us understand the phenomenon in new and useful ways.

This form of analysis is very clearly based on the assumption that there is a performance going on and that the performance is influencing the meaning of the actions taken by the actors. While this assumption is often true (Goffman, 1959, 1974), it may not always be and it may not be a useful way to perceive the phenomenon. These decisions must be left to the researchers who are familiar with the settings and with the purpose of their interpretations.

The brevity of this chapter should not be taken to imply that I consider dramaturgical analysis to be either less important or simpler than the other theories. Indeed, the work of Goffman, alone, is sufficient to convince one of the dizzying possibilities of dramaturgical analysis. This book, however, is intended to provide an introduction to the theories and the resulting analytical approach. Many features of the dramaturgical analysis are already somewhat familiar to most readers through their consumption of popular media. This distinguishes this theory from the other theories presented in this book, which may be familiar only in name to many readers. This familiarity means that less information is required for an adequate introduction to the approach. It may also mean that dramaturgy is more accessible to many readers though it is certainly no less revelatory as a result.

NOTE

1. These complaints did decrease over the four years of observation. I am not sure, however, if I heard fewer complaints because there were fewer complaints or because the building directors had already spoken at length to me about them or for some other reason.

5. DECONSTRUCTION

Deconstruction is a process that rests on several assumptions. The first is that ideology imposes limits on what can and cannot be said. The second is that most authors write and actors act from within an ideology. Therefore their texts and actions are bound by the limits of their ideology. Deconstruction as an analytical tool aims at exposing these ideological limits. "Deconstruction turns attention to how language creates some meanings and suppresses other meanings" (Manning, 1992, pp. 203-204). "Deconstruction is a means to see words in context and to examine the effects of changing contexts on meaning" (Manning, 1992, p. 202).

Deconstruction is accomplished through several specific ways of looking at a text (a verbal exchange or an action). These ways of looking are often called moves. Some of the most common include looking at what is not said or looking at silences and gaps, dismantling dichotomies, and analyzing disruptions. Joanne Martin, in her article "Deconstructing Organizational Taboos" (1990), provides an excellent description, explanation, and illustration of these and other moves used in deconstruction. The example I use later in this chapter illustrates each of the three moves. Here I describe them briefly.

In any text, verbal exchange, or action, what is written, said, or done is a "selective and partial representation" (Manning, 1992, p. 202). It can be interpreted according to what is written, said, or done, but it can also be interpreted according to what is not written, said, or done. A humorous version of interpreting what is not done is represented by the joke about the mother who gives her son two ties for his birthday. When he appears later in the day wearing one of the ties, she wants to know why he doesn't like the other tie. A less humorous version occurs in performance evaluations and recommendation letters in which what is not said may be more telling than what is said. The notion of damning with faint praise is another commonly known example of this phenomenon. One of the moves of deconstruction is to notice what is not said, or at least some of what is not said, even in situations in which the tendency is to focus on what is said.

Dichotomies divide the world into two categories. Common dichotomies are public and private, men and women, us and them, good and bad. Because dichotomies allow for only two possibilities, they tend to restrict the kinds of questions that are asked. If, for instance, we assume that everyone can be classified as either a man or a woman, then we rule out of existence, or at least out of our consciousness, the possibility of people with ambiguous sex identities (Geertz, 1983). Likewise, when we assume that the dichotomy is relevant (for instance, to the division of labor), we privilege the characteristics of the categories over the characteristics of individuals. We may become unable to see that people in different categories may have very similar characteristics. Similarly, if we assume that a matter is either public or private, then we make it considerably more difficult to deal with the implications for work (a public affair) of a person's family life (a private affair) (Martin, 1990). One of the moves of deconstruction is to be aware of dichotomies and to ask the questions that tend to be ignored because of the dichotomy.

The Freudian slip is probably the most widely known example of a disruption. A slip of the tongue is interpreted from the Freudian perspective as meaningful and not just as an accident. Similarly, a thought that is not completed, a great deal of hesitation before expressing a thought, sentences that start out going in one direction but end up in another, and so forth can all be interpreted as meaningful. The meaning attributed to these disruptions in the smooth flow of text, talk, or action depends upon the contexts, and it is up to the researcher engaging in deconstruction to make a convincing connection between the disruption and the interpretation of it.

I have seen deconstruction used to reveal either the ideology of a particular culture or the ideology of the analysts of a culture (which is, of course, a culture in itself). Carol Cohn (1987), for example, examines the language, jargon, and acronyms of the world of nuclear defense to reveal the images of sex and death in a culture that claims to be objective, distant, and rational. She goes further to show that the language these people use to talk about the life-and-death concerns their work involves places boundaries on how these concerns can be thought about and acted upon. Finally, she shows how the language also delegitimizes, and therefore silences, people who may think differently about these issues.

Renato Rosaldo, by contrast, uses deconstruction techniques to show how categories used by analysts of culture systematically restrict the analysts' view of the culture they study. In his book *Culture and Truth* (1989), he examines the ideologies that suggest that chaos and social structure are opposites (chap. 4) and that time is a matter of segmentation and sequencing (chap. 5). Rather than deconstruct the ideologies of the people he studies (though he may do this in other texts), he deconstructs the ideology of the analysts. He helps us to see how, for example, by focusing on clock time, we tend to see more of the external features of events rather than their internal dynamics.

Deconstruction began in the field of literary criticism and was originally a way of analyzing texts. As it has been adopted by the social sciences, it has still been associated primarily with texts. Speeches (Martin, 1990), articles (Calás, 1992; Calás & Smirchich, 1989, 1992), judicial proceedings (Scheppele, 1990, 1992), and automatic teller machine messages (Manning, 1992) are examples of texts that have been deconstructed. When deconstruction is used to analyze action, some people refer to this as "textualizing the action" (Calás, personal conversation, 1992, July 16). While I have seen deconstructions of such disparate phenomena as baseball caps (Manning, 1992) and the analysis of a visit in the Ilongot culture (Rosaldo, 1989), it is easiest for me to illustrate deconstruction using a "text." Thus, although many of the issues I have discussed in this book are amenable to deconstruction—such as the notion of building or the idea of building a community—I introduce a slightly new topic for this analysis. The issue is hierarchical power and the "text" is a segment of conversation from a meeting of several building directors, an assistant director, and the associate director of Residence Education.

Analysis

I found it very difficult to do this deconstruction. It is possible that part of the problem in deconstructing the ideology of Residence Education is that Residence Education presents itself as a postmodern organization.

That is, members of Residence Education believe in and consciously work at replacing dualism with duality. Dualism suggests that the world can be divided into black and white, public and private, rational and nonrational, and that these "opposites" neither necessitate one another nor commingle in any significant way. Duality suggests that the "opposites" are related as two sides of a coin—one implies the other; one cannot exist without the other; the boundaries of each are thoroughly permeated by the other.

Take, for example, the issue of hierarchy. A traditional view might suggest that people are either equal or not equal. Equality does not imply inequality or vice versa; the two are simply separate and distinct qualities. One is a superior, a peer, or a subordinate. A nondualistic view of hierarchy might be that position is contextual, that being superior or subordinate depends on the answer to the question: "At what?" In Residence Education, for example, central administrators dominate in policymaking while building directors dominate with respect to the day-to-day activities in their buildings.

Just as gender is important to maintaining separate realms of domination for men and woman (e.g., men are good at fighting and women are good at nurturing) and, in some real sense, people give up a source of power by preferring not to divide realms, the building directors would sacrifice their source of power if they gave up the building/central administration distinction. The notion that buildings are separate realms with distinct "personalities" gives building-level managers a well-defined area of expertise. The expertise gives them authority and therefore power. The expertise means that, in many situations, decision-making power is delegated to the building-level managers. The extent of this delegation reaches its height in Residence Education, in which the building is defined not by physical structures and materials but by people and social relations. Information about the former is much easier to relay and decays less rapidly than information about the latter. It is, for instance, easier to consult among others in the hierarchy about a roof that is about to collapse than about a person who is about to commit suicide. Both cases constitute crises, but in the case of the roof there can be a standard procedure for evacuating the area, inspecting the damage, and assessing what action should be taken. While standard procedures exist for handling suicides, the situation is considerably more volatile and each instance is different. These are both extreme cases, but they serve to illustrate why there is a greater need for delegation and discretionary power at the building level in Residence Education than in either Facilities or Food Service.

Thus the claim that central administration people are, in some sense, equals or peers to the building-level people can be maintained within Residence Education. Yet that claim is contradicted in many ways. The people at the central administration level make more money, can override decisions made at the building level, and can require building-level people to take certain actions. The central administration people regularly review the performance of building-level people and recommend their salary increases. While access to information about salaries is available to everyone because the Housing Department is part of a state university, it is the business of the central administrators to know the salaries of the building-level managers and not vice versa. Central administrators approve or disapprove of projects requiring over $1,000. Central administrators control resources though they depend on building-level people for information about how to use them.

The ideology that everyone is equal with different domains of expertise is also maintained within the buildings across functional areas. This is quite evident in the reserves process in which the building-level managers are urged by central administrators to produce consensus lists of reserves projects. The assumption of equality ignores the considerable differences in traditional sources of power—education, salary, physical location in building, type of work (blue collar versus white collar), secretarial support, and so forth.

This ideology creates both problems and opportunities for both hierarchical superiors and hierarchical subordinates. In some ways, the ideology is self-serving for the hierarchical superiors. They are relieved of the need to manage the inequities among building-level managers. They are relieved, at least somewhat, of the need to legitimate their own positions. They are able to discuss the institutional setting with their hierarchical subordinates without the onus of being more responsible for it than the subordinates are. The hierarchical subordinates meanwhile maintain the illusion of power and, indeed, maintain some real power in their limited domains. The disadvantages of the ideology may be more clear after the analysis of a segment of conversation that was taped during a meeting about a report on the role of building directors. It is about compensation levels, or salaries. It reflects some of these issues concerning equality/inequality in Residence Education. I discuss the conversation after the transcription.

Helene: [1] One of the areas in here under the personnel . . . one of the areas we talked about last time we were here—

Ned: yep—um

Helene: the personnel committee within these little building committee things that is um basically um—Pearl and Nadine and me?

Patricia: Vicky

Helene: Pearl and Vicky and me—thank you um — some of the things we are working out with that group will eventually have an impact on these reports and you'll get some of that too. . . . so there's more

Ned: can you give me some clues?

Helene: let's see—one of the three goals or whatever that we are supposed to accomplish within six weeks—or six months—or what was the topic the last time we broke into small groups—six weeks?

Patricia: yeah six months I think

Helene: six months?

Pearl: was it six months?

Helene: —I thought there was one that was six weeks—anyway—what we talked about was compensation levels across P & A[2] levels—not within the Resed group but . . . .

Patricia: within housing

Helene: just to kno:::w[3] and we're working on tha:::t and also some information that has to do with other institutions and we'll—that committee's working on that

Patricia: their compensation?

Helene: right—it just so happens that Pearl and I are on this and that committee but Vicky is the additional member

Ned: Pullman and I have been saving some stuff on compensational things— you might want to talk to him about that

Helene: well Nancy Jacobson was very helpful to me—she gave me lists of names that I knew and I've had my secretary working on—for instance, take a P & A 8 across facilities, food service, administration, Rese:::d and to track salary levels and longevity and um what I need now is to find somebody who has the ability to know how to do graphics on a computer to do charts cause the IBM won't do that the way I need it to

Ned: um—if you also . . I have university averages. . . . . I have . . . .

Helene: for job categories?

Ned: yup and the unit . . . average years in position . . . some of those things you might find useful

Helene: I would think I would not know what to do with that at this point, but in two months I will

Patricia: Penny O'Neal was helpful—I mean she put our chart together for the BD role report—I don't know what she's doing . . . if she might be available but she. . .

Helene: OK

Ned: I would imagine that Williams ought to be able to help with some of this

Helene: well in a month I'll ask her. I know I can't do anything other than delegate things to my secretary real quickly right now

Ned: yeah. . . . I . . . I understand what you are getting at here too and it's a it's an interesting one um . . . . just as an example and my guess is that it might be the same for some of you. . . . I . . . . I . . . . I get umm . . . . my compensation is virtually twice what it was when I came here six years ago—not quite—um . . . . and yet I um . . . .at that point I was at the mid-point of my P & A range and now I'm at the 38th percentile

?: Gee

Pearl: an' I've been here for 11 years and I'm not doubled and so I've got to be way down in the quartile

Ned: yah

Pearl: yah

Helene: there's a lot of different ways of looking at that—tha:::t's one and another is to take like a set of seven and to look at it across job family to look at uh . . . .lots of different you know to be able to put it on a program and have it turn graphs on like five different areas

Ned: that will be useful

Helene: we will learn a lot about the computer doing it—I've already learned a lot . . . .I mean a lot compared to what I'm used to

Ned: um . . . .

Patricia: I . . . .

Ned: go ahead please

Patricia: I remember during our last meeting that . . . . (she begins discussing another issue).

Much of the discussion makes sense as a conversation among peers. It suggests a peer relationship in many ways. First, the building directors are putting together information about compensation levels outside of their own unit to legitimate their own requests for change in compensation. This is a task often taken on by one's hierarchical superior. Ned offers to provide information that he and another person (Pullman) have been gathering. One can imagine a conversation between peers in two different units who are both investigating compensation levels and offering to help one another out. Then Ned comments about his compensation level and how it has changed since he was hired. One meaning of the remark is that people in that unit are disadvantaged in their compensation levels vis-à-vis other groups around the university in the same P & A level. It may be seen both as a guess about what is happening to them and as a request for information about whether the same thing is really happening to all of them. Finally, Helene says that the sort of comparison that Ned and Pearl are engaged in is just one sort of comparison and that there are lots of other analyses that need to be done.

This conversation, however, does not take place among peers. Present at the meeting were four building directors, one assistant director of Residence Education, and the associate director of Residence Education. (I was not present, the meeting was taped for me in my absence.) Only four people spoke during the transcribed segment of the meeting. They were Helene (a building director), Patricia (an assistant director for Residence Education), Ned (the associate director for Residence Education), and Pearl (a building director).

Ned's comment about his compensation level may be understood quite differently in this context. Ned is hierarchically superior and has a higher salary. Furthermore, his salary was almost certainly higher before it doubled. Three of the five other people in the meeting were in Residence Education when Ned was hired and they are all his subordinates. One of them, Pearl, comments that her salary *hasn't* doubled in the *eleven* years she has been in Residence Education. This salary difference mitigates the interpretation proposed by Ned that they are all in a disadvantaged group. Instead, it seems to draw attention to the fact that some in this group are substantially more disadvantaged than others, as evidenced by Pearl's response to Ned's example.

The interpretation that Ned is making a guess about what is happening to the group and possibly fishing for information, which is supported by his comment "and my guess is that it might be the same for some of you," is also contradicted when the context is considered. In fact, it is Ned's job not only to know but also to set the salaries of the people in the room. While he does not have total control over salary levels because he is constrained by university regulations and by budget restrictions, he does have substantially more control than any one else in the room. He also has ready access to the information he claims to be guessing about. While it may be true that he did not check the information prior to the meeting and therefore isn't sure about it when he speaks, he certainly doesn't have to guess about the truth of this claim.

The other people in the meeting were complicit in maintaining the notion that everyone is equal. With the exceptions of Pearl's comment about her salary and Ned's example, the entire discussion of compensation is very academic. Much of the discussion has to do with how the research will be done rather than with the specific topic. One notable instance of this focus occurs after Ned's example and Pearl's comment when Helene pulls the conversation back by asserting that the focus Ned and Pearl have taken is just one of many ways to look at the issue.

As Helene brings the discussion back to a more dispassionate tone, she returns to the issue of using computer graphics, which has been another major focal point of the discussion to this point. In fact, computers were discussed previously in this meeting. The previous discussion was about whether building directors should use IBMs or Macintoshes. The building/central administration distinction is central to this discussion. Ned favors the use of IBMs for the building directors because that is what the central administrators use and compatibility facilitates sharing of reports and other documents. The building directors tend to favor Macintoshes because the people who report to them (resident directors and advisors) use Macs and because the increased ability for graphics and free-form drawing supports their computer needs more effectively. The building directors' position is consistent with the notion that the buildings are autonomous while Ned's position is consistent with the notion that the buildings are not autonomous. Helene's concern about the need for graphics indirectly engages this previous discussion by highlighting her current inability to do what she wants to do.

The computer focus also emphasizes the "objective" nature of the conversation: that all that is going on now is analysis. This has two effects. One is to reassert the technical or cool aspect of the discussion. Helene needs computer graphics to show the many different ways it is possible to look at this issue. She presents herself as not having any particular ax to grind, but simply information to analyze. The other effect is to postpone the time of any potential conflict. In essence, Helene is saying that all that is happening now is analysis, and we will have to wait until some future time to know if the analysis will lead to any action.

Summary

The major focus of this deconstruction has been the dichotomy of hierarchical superior and subordinate. Of the moves described at the beginning of this chapter, the focus has been on dismantling a dichotomy. The deconstruction has not exactly been a dismantling of the dichotomy because the ideology of the Residence Education culture is to obscure the distinction between hierarchical levels. The analysis has, instead, emphasized the efforts made to ignore the differences between hierarchical superiors and subordinates. It is important here for me to be clear that I am not saying that either ideology—the one that ignores hierarchical distinctions or the one that dwells on them—is more in tune with "reality." One can find support for either perspective. The point is that either perspective limits what people say and do. In this case, the deconstruction focuses on how the efforts to ignore hierarchical differences limit discussion.

There are also silences and gaps in this conversation. For instance, no one says specifically that they are unhappy about compensation levels. The person who comes the closest to saying this is Ned, the boss. But he is talking about his own salary. Given that this is a meeting of several building directors with their boss to talk about the building director position, it seems like a fine time to say, "We don't think we get paid enough." Of course, it is possible that this is already obvious or perceived to be obvious. One can imagine a number of other topics that could be raised about compensation in a meeting with one's boss. For instance, one could ask about the process for changing salaries; one could ask about the boss's assessment of the prospects of change and what one could do to increase these prospects; one could ask about what information the boss has and what other information needs to be gathered; one could ask about the boss's support for an increase. I am sure you can add to this list.

While the issue of information does arise, the building directors do not appear to be asking advice of their boss but informing him of what they are doing. The boss offers some help at this point, mentioning some information he has been gathering, and the help is temporarily refused. ("Helene: I would think I would not know what to do with that at this point, but in two months I will . . .") The other issues are not raised.

There are many other issues that are raised and receive considerable attention. The people who are on the committee come up twice in this brief excerpt; whether the time line is six weeks or six months is the topic of five entries. These two topics come up at the beginning of the discussion and it takes a while even to figure out what is being discussed. When the topic is first introduced, there is so much ambiguity about what is discussed that Ned finally asks, "Can you give me some clues?" A few entries later, Patricia clarifies again that the discussion is about compensation. In all, it takes more than one third of the entries in this excerpt to establish the topic. Once the topic is firmly established, the issue of computers becomes important. It is a way of talking about the topic without talking specifically about salaries.

The effort not to confront the issue of salaries directly is made more clear through a comment that can be seen as a disruption. The statement is the one made by Ned about his compensation level. In making this comment, Ned asserts both his solidarity and his dominance. Discussion of his compensation level (which everyone knows is higher) creates an opening to acknowledge hierarchical differences. He says:

yeah . . . . I . . . I understand what you are getting at here too and it's a it's an interesting one um . . . . just as an example and my guess is that it might be the same for some of you . . . . I . . . . I . . . . I get umm . . . .my compensation is virtually twice what it was when I came here six years ago—not quite—um . . . . and yet I um . . . .at that point I was at the mid-point of my P & A range and now I'm at the 38th percentile.

His speech (". . . I . . . I . . . I get umm . . . my") suggests his hesitation about creating this opening. But he nonetheless goes ahead. The remark is met with silence, then a stunned "Gee." The opening is taken up by Pearl, who says "an' I've been here for 11 years and I'm not doubled and so I've got to be way down in the quartile." Ned and Pearl then encourage one another with a round of "yah," but neither is willing to take the next step. At this point, Helene steps in to pull the conversation away from the brink of acknowledging hierarchical differences by reminding them that "there's a lot of different ways of looking at that . . ." The disruption helps us to see both the limit and the effort that goes into avoiding a breach of this limit.

Though it is not a deconstructive move, there is one other move that I made in doing this analysis that was very helpful. When I transcribed the text of the conversation, I changed the names of the participants. This is a simple but powerful move. As I discuss shortly, one of the difficulties of deconstruction, and indeed of all analysis of qualitative data, is the need to separate oneself emotionally from a context in which one has spent a lot of time. Names help to maintain the attachment in a mysterious but powerful way. Changing the names helps to create some separation.

Reflection on Deconstruction

Of the methods of analyzing qualitative data presented here, this deconstruction is clearly the most difficult for me. The difficulty I experience is also one of the main reasons this method is so valuable. Deconstruction forces one to confront the ideology of the culture, to look through the holes in it, and to see how it differs from what it purports to be. It is the art of announcing that the emperor has no clothes. When one is looking in from the outside of a culture, possibly even a culture one does not particularly like, the task is one of intellectual difficulty. When one has spent considerable time in a culture, has been accepted in some sense as an "honorary member," and has been trusted and confided in, the task may also entail substantial emotional and psychological difficulty.

Immersing oneself in a culture often involves considerable trust for both the researcher and the researched.[4] While people doing qualitative research in their own country do not generally eat and sleep with the people they study, dependencies and attachments do develop. The researcher comes to know the people she studies. Being entrusted with feelings, opinions, and information creates links between human beings. But the researcher cannot know without also being known. One does, of course, keep one's feelings and opinions to oneself as much as possible. As day follows day, however, one changes, has moods, goes through periods of stress when other parts of one's life make the research either more difficult or a welcome relief. Even if these changes, moods, feelings are never discussed, they are experienced in the presence of others creating a certain vulnerability and the opportunity for trust and attachment. The research site in this sense becomes a home; that is, it is a place where one lives even if only on certain days of the week or between certain hours of the day. While there is no doubt that one has to leave this home, disengagement is not necessarily easy.

Deconstruction pushes one beyond physical disengagement to intellectual and emotional disengagement. The researcher not only leaves the research site but also begins to view the culture from a distance. Ways of seeing that had become familiar and comfortable must become unfamiliar. What one has come to see as reasonable approaches to problems and issues in the setting one must be capable of seeing as absurd, distasteful, or exploitative. People one has come to enjoy, be fond of, and trust may be revealed as denying reality for their own gain or simply ignorant of the intense biases of their ideology. The desire not to offend may pose substantial obstacles to using deconstruction on certain aspects of the culture or at all.

I encourage use of this technique for exactly the reasons that it may be difficult or painful. The exercise of forcing oneself to view the culture from a different perspective is invaluable to interpretive work. Deconstruction is one of the quickest and surest means I know to achieve this end. While the perspective developed through deconstruction may not be the ultimate basis for an interpretation, it makes the researcher more aware of her or his subjectivity and can, as a result, open the research to a wider array of understandings.

The statement above that deconstruction is one of the quickest means I know to achieve a new perspective on a setting should not be taken to imply that deconstruction is a shortcut to doing fieldwork. Gaining a new perspective requires that one first have a perspective to move away from. One of the purposes of fieldwork is to understand as well as possible the perspectives of the members of the culture.[5] Once one views the culture as nearly as possible through the eyes of a member, the deconstruction helps to illuminate how his or her perspectives limit his or her ideas and options. Unless one starts from this "member's" perspective, the deconstruction may not reveal much about the members' ideologies.

Remember that deconstruction assumes that there is an implicit ideology that limits the speech and actions of the members of the culture. The purpose of deconstruction is to expose the ideological limits.

NOTES

1. The names in this passage have been changed.
2. "P & A" stands for Professional and Administrative and the levels are a way of classifying jobs for personnel purposes.

3. The punctuation on this word indicates that the speaker elongated the vowel in pronouncing the word. This punctuation is used throughout the transcript.
4. See Adler and Adler (1987), Lofland and Lofland (1984), and Wax (1971) for excellent discussions of the issues of involvement, trust, and memberships in fieldwork.
5. One must recognize that there is no one perspective or ideology held by all members.

6. CONCLUSION

Role of Analysis

Throughout this book, I have assumed that analysis is just one stage in the process of research. It is preceded by data gathering and succeeded by a process of relating one's interpretations to the questions one is trying to answer and to existing theories. In the case of qualitative research, it is often easy to blur the stages. It is important, however, to keep them as separate as possible. It is tempting not to separate the data gathering from the analysis. If one were to adopt an analytical framework prior to gathering data, it could greatly simplify and possibly shorten the data gathering process. One must, however, resist this temptation. Succumbing to it may considerably reduce the effectiveness of the research as it may reduce the ability of the researcher to understand the relevant phenomena from the perspectives of the members of the culture.

One must also be clear that the interpretations that result from the analysis are not the "final" interpretation unless, of course, the question being answered is this: "What kind of culture is this?" Analysis is a process that facilitates these "final" interpretations. Interpreting is an activity that we all engage in on a daily basis. Some people are better at it than others, but anyone who communicates with others makes interpretations. The difficulty in interpreting qualitative data is not in learning how to create interpretations but in learning how to get away from preestablished interpretations. There are two main sorts of preestablished interpretation that are difficult to avoid. One is the interpretations made by people in the setting being studied. The other is the interpretations made by other researchers and theorists about phenomena similar to the ones under study. Anyone doing qualitative research will have a great deal of knowledge of both sorts of interpretations. Indeed, this knowledge is essential. It is also essential, however, to be able to move away from this knowledge and to be able to gain new understandings of the phenomena reflected in the data. The techniques described in this monograph can be used to produce this effect.

Appropriate Uses of the Techniques

I have described four theories and illustrated techniques for analyzing qualitative data that derive from these theories. The examples in this text of the use of the techniques should be considered illustrative rather than definitive. In each case, I am aware that I could have continued use of the technique to explore a particular issue more deeply or to examine other, related issues. My illustrations are intended to elicit interest in the techniques and to provide a starting point that can be further elaborated by other researchers.

These techniques are each useful in allowing the researcher to gain new insights into the phenomena she or he is investigating. They do this primarily by encouraging the researcher to go behind the surface understandings through the use of assumptions and categories associated with the assumptions. Thus deconstruction encourages the researcher to look for the underlying "reality" or ideology while ethnomethodology urges the researcher to find out how the "reality" is constructed. Semiotics motivates the researcher to find the structure connecting the surface manifestations (signs) with the underlying meanings (signifieds). Dramaturgical analysis impels one to look for the performance and meanings generated by the performance.

My use of these techniques to analyze different aspects of my data may raise questions about the appropriate use of the techniques. While throughout the text I have emphasized the importance of being attentive to the assumptions implicit in the ideas underlying the techniques, I have not been explicit about why I have chosen to use a particular technique in a particular instance. This is not a question that has an easy answer. The choice to use one technique rather than or along with another is heavily dependent on the data one has and the issues one is interested in exploring. A thorough understanding of the appropriate uses of the techniques is probably best developed through experience, and I encourage people interested in these techniques to experiment. In the following discussion, I attempt to provide some ways of thinking about which technique might be appropriate for any particular data or issue. I do this by talking about certain tendencies in the sets of ideas and the ways they have been used.

It is important to understand that the categories I use are in no way absolute and that taking them too seriously will result in inadequate understanding of the ideas and inappropriate uses of the techniques.

One way to describe these techniques involves whether they emphasize process (how) or outcome (what). Of course, all of the techniques deal to some extent with both process and outcome. Ethnomethodology, however, has process as its primary focus while dramaturgy and deconstruction tend to be more outcome oriented. Ethnomethodology focuses on how an outcome occurs. Dramaturgy and deconstruction focus more on what is happening or what has happened. Where interpretations are concerned, ethnomethodology is attentive to how the interpretation came to be; dramaturgy and deconstruction are attentive to what the interpretation consists of. Semiotics analyses may focus on either what or how. In my examples, the first and third semiotic techniques focus on "what" issues while the second emphasizes "how" issues.

Another perspective on these ideas is provided by viewing the extent to which they tend to be used to deal specifically with power and dominance. Deconstruction and dramaturgy are often used to deal with these issues. Deconstruction focuses attention on the dominant ideology and is often used to show how alternate interpretations are delegitimated. Dramaturgy tends to focus on people and groups within the society who have access to resources and who use these resources to invoke and manipulate meaning. There is nothing intrinsic to dramaturgical analysis that promotes this tendency except that people with power tend to have more attention paid to their performances and thus tend to have a greater ability to influence interpretations. It is for this reason, I believe, that dramaturgical analyses are inclined to focus on people with power and on issues of power and dominance.

Ethnomethodologists, by contrast, seldom focus on issues of power and dominance. The emphasis within this set of ideas is on negotiation and on the mutual need to maintain shared meanings. Thus ethnomethodologists tend not to discuss the extent to which the meanings advantage one group over another. This is consistent with the ethnomethodological emphasis on process over outcome. The process is presumably the same regardless of whom the outcome benefits.

Two of the techniques focus more on the stability of meaning while the other two focus on the instability or malleability of meaning. Ethnomethodology and semiotics are similar in that they emphasize stability. Heritage

(1984), for instance, describes the outcome of Garfinkel's early experiments in ethnomethodology as showing the extreme difficulty of disrupting intersubjective understandings. "The 'chess-board' of meaning is revealed to be self-righting. The normative accountability of action is thus a seamless web, an endless metric in terms of which conduct is unavoidably intelligible, describable and assessable" (Garfinkel, 1984, p. 100). Semiotics, with its emphasis on deep structure being manifest through surface phenomena, also tends to focus attention on the stability of meaning. Even when the surface manifestations change, the deep structure is seldom affected so that the overall meaning is unchanged.

By contrast, deconstruction focuses specifically on the instability of meaning. The importance of disruptions, gaps, and silences is that they show that other meanings are persistently poking through the fabric of the dominant ideology. The ability to deconstruct established categorizations is based on the fragility of meaning. Dramaturgy also draws attention to the instability of meaning by emphasizing its malleability. The drama is a means of invoking meaning and can be orchestrated. Thus dramaturgical analysis increases our awareness of the fluidity of meaning.

This discussion of the stability and instability of meaning provides a good opportunity for reflecting on the adequacy and the appropriate use of these ways of categorizing the techniques. While categories are useful for sorting things, we must recognize that they simultaneously produce false differentiation. The focus on the stability or instability of meaning made it appropriate to separate ethnomethodology from deconstruction. From another perspective, however, these two techniques are not opposites but simply two sides of the same coin. In both ethnomethodology and deconstruction, the notion of a hole in the fabric of meaning is important. In ethnomethodology, this is referred to as a breach, and it is thought to happen infrequently because of the constant work people engage in to keep meaning ongoing. In deconstruction, disruptions are breaks in the taken-for-granted ideology. They are thought to occur frequently and are indicators of the instability of meaning. Both sets of ideas are concerned with a similar phenomenon. From one perspective (deconstruction), the concern is with the breaking up; from the other perspective (ethnomethodology), the concern is with the repair process. Thus, even though the techniques are quite different with respect to their take on the stability of meaning, they may be fruitfully used to analyze the same data and the same issues.

The techniques may often be used in combination with one another. One technique may be used to show aspects of the data that the other does not emphasize, or one technique may be used to elaborate another. For instance, both the ethnomethodology and the semiotics analyses helped me focus on the centrality of the building concept. One helped me identify it while the other helped me develop the connection of it to other issues of concern in the organization. Both the semiotic squares and the dramaturgical analysis helped me understand different aspects of the budgeting process. The semiotic squares, the dramaturgical analysis, and the deconstruction all led me to new perspectives on the issue of hierarchy in the Housing Department and Residence Education. Together the techniques substantially broadened and deepened my understanding of the culture of the organization and provided a base for future interpretations.

I hope this text helps you to experiment with the techniques and to explore your data. Try using several techniques on the same data or different aspects of the same data set. See what understandings emerge. Just remember that, as with any analytic technique, the analysis is not an end in itself but an aid to the ultimate process of interpretation.

I began this book with an observation about the huge amount of data one has after completing the data gathering process in a qualitative research project and how difficult it is to figure out how to begin to create interpretations from all these data. I must admit that, after engaging in all of the analytical techniques, I still have piles and piles of data to explore. There is a difference, however. I have a much better understanding of the culture from which these data come. When I read my notes or listen to a tape or read someone's electronic mail, I have new ways of understanding these data. The data gathering process changed my perspective from that of an outsider to more of an insider. The analysis process helped me to be able to view that insider's perspective without losing the knowledge that I gained from it. This new understanding helps me to ask different questions and develop different interpretations. I can now go beyond seeing the research site from the members' perspectives and work at developing interpretations that are revealing and informative to both insiders and outsiders.

REFERENCES

Adler, P. A., & Adler, P. (1987). *Membership roles in field research.* Newbury Park, CA: Sage.

Agar, M. H. (1980). *The professional stranger: An informal introduction to ethnography.* Orlando, FL: Academic Press.

Barley, S. R. (1983). Semiotics and the study of occupational and organizational culture. *Administrative Science Quarterly, 28,* 393-413.

Barthes, R. (1972). *Mythologies.* New York: Hill and Wang.

Barthes, R. (1982). *Empire of signs.* New York: Hill and Wang.

Bennett, W. L., & Feldman, M. S. (1981). *Reconstructing reality in the courtroom.* New Brunswick, NJ: Rutgers University Press.

Building director role report. (1989). Unpublished report.

Burke, K. (1969). *A grammar of motives.* Berkeley: University of California Press.

Calás, M. (1992). An/other silent voice? Representing 'Hispanic woman' in organizational texts. In A. J. Mills & P. Tancred (Eds.), *Gendering organization theory* (pp. 201-221). Newbury Park, CA: Sage.

Calás, M., & Smirchich, L. (1989). Using the "F" word: Feminist theories and the social consequences of organizational research. In *Academy of Management best papers proceedings* (pp. 355-359). Washington, DC: Academy of Management.

Calás, M., & Smirchich, L. (1992). Rewriting gender into organization theorizing: Directions from feminist perspectives. In M. I. Reed & M. D. Hughes (Eds.), *Re-thinking organization: New directions in organizational research and analysis* (pp. 227-253). London: Sage.

Clifford, J. (1986). Partial truths. In J. Clifford & G. E. Marcus (Eds.), *Writing culture* (pp. 1-26). Berkeley: University of California Press.

Cohn, C. (1987). Sex and death in the rational world of defense intellectuals. *Signs: Journal of Women in Culture and Society, 12,* 687-718.

Eco, U. (1976). *A theory of semiotics.* Bloomington: University of Indiana Press.

Enomoto, E. (1993). *In-school truancy in a multiethnic urban high school examined through organizational culture laws.* Unpublished doctoral dissertation, University of Michigan.

Feldman, M. S. (forthcoming). *Organizational routines as practice.*

Fiol, C. M. (1989). A semiotic analysis of corporate language: Organizational boundaries and joint venturing. *Administrative Science Quarterly, 34,* 277-303.

Garfinkel, H. (1967). *Studies in ethnomethodology.* Cambridge: Polity.

Geertz, C. (1983). *Local knowledge: Further essays in interpretive anthropology.* New York: Basic Books.

Goffman, I. (1959). *The presentation of self in everyday life.* New York: Doubleday.

Goffman, I. (1967). *Interaction ritual.* New York: Pantheon.

Goffman, I. (1974). *Frame analysis.* Boston: Northeastern University Press.

Greimas, A. (1987). *On meaning.* Minneapolis: University of Minnesota Press.

Heritage, J. (1984). *Garfinkel and ethnomethodology.* Cambridge: Polity.

Lofland, J., & Lofland, L. H. (1984). *Analyzing social settings.* Belmont, CA: Wadsworth.

Manning, P. K. (1977). *Police work: The social organization of policing.* Cambridge: MIT Press.

70

Manning, P. K. (1987). *Semiotics and fieldwork.* Newbury Park, CA: Sage.
Manning, P. K. (1992). *Organizational communication.* New York: Aldine de Greyter.
Martin, J. (1990). Deconstructing organizational taboos: The suppression of gender conflict in organizations. *Organizational Science, 1*(4), 339-359.
Martin, J., Feldman, M. S., Hatch, M. J., & Sitkin, S. B. (1983). The uniqueness paradox in organizational stories. *Administrative Science Quarterly, 28,* 438-453.
Mulkay, M., & Gilbert, G. N. (1983). Scientists' theory talk. *Canadian Journal of Sociology, 8,* 179-187.
Rosaldo, R. (1989). *Culture and truth.* Boston: Beacon.
Scheppele, K. (1990). Facing facts in legal interpretation. *Representations, 30,* 42-77.
Scheppele, K. (1992). Just the facts ma'am: Sexualized violence, evidentiary habits and the revision of truth. *New York Law School Law Review, 37,* 123-172.
Spradley, J. P. (1979). *The ethnographic interview.* Fortworth, TX: Holt, Rinehart & Winston.
Suchman, L. A. (1987). *Plans and situated actions.* Cambridge, MA: Cambridge University Press.
Wax, R. H. (1971). *Doing fieldwork: Warnings and advice.* Chicago: University of Chicago Press.

ABOUT THE AUTHOR

MARTHA S. FELDMAN is Associate Professor of Political Science and Public Policy at the University of Michigan, Ann Arbor. Her research interests involve how people construct their social reality and how they act in a social context. Her particular focus has been on organizational decision making and how various forms of information and communication are involved in that process. She is currently studying organizational routines as a form of practice. This approach emphasizes the importance of context in interpreting behavior and the way in which behavior produces and reproduces organizational structure. Her publications include *Order Without Design: Information Production and Policy Making, Reconstructing Reality in the Courtroom* (coauthored with W. Lance Bennett), and *Information in Organizations as Signal and Symbol* (coauthored with James G. March).